All the best

ADVANCE ACCLAIM FOR

THREE CORDS APPROACH TO LIFE AND WEALTH MANAGEMENT FOR BUSINESS OWNERS

"Congratulations to Rocco on writing a book that details the exact strategy to maximizing our financial lives. Get ready to stop stressing about money and finally live life on your terms."

—Mike Michalowicz

Author, Clockwork *and* Profit First

"Rocco teaches leaders that they need to exhibit a trinity of strength: in understanding self, business, and family. Yet finding that sweet spot in the balancing act is the common frustration for most self-aware, entrepreneurial family men and women. If we don't want to wake up at the end of our lives and wonder where our satisfaction, money, and relationships have gone, we'll take this engaging book to heart and put its truths into action."

—Tim Thayne, PhD, LMFT

Author, Not by Chance: How Parents Boost Their Teen's Success In and After Treatment

"One of my favorite quotations comes from Johann Wolfgang von Goethe, 'Things which matter most must never be at the mercy of things which matter least.' Rocco A. Carriero, in his book, Three Cords Approach to Life and Wealth Management for Business Owners, *masterfully shares solutions that will help you achieve those things that truly matter most to you. Inspired by actual stories, concepts, principles, and tools tested in the trenches, this book will arm you with greater clarity and direction in today's unsettling times. You may want to read the last chapter first. It inspired me to soak up every word."*

—Lee M. Brower

Founder of Empowered Wealth, LC and Global Cultural Artist to Entrepreneurial Family Businesses

Author, The Brower Quadrant

ROCCO A. CARRIERO

THREE CORDS

APPROACH

TO LIFE AND WEALTH MANAGEMENT FOR BUSINESS OWNERS

ForbesBooks

Published by ForbesBooks, Charleston, South Carolina.
Member of Advantage Media Group.

ForbesBooks is a registered trademark, and the ForbesBooks colophon is a trademark of Forbes Media, LLC.

Printed in the United States of America.

10 9 8 7 6 5 4 3 2 1

ISBN: 978-1-946633-08-8
LCCN: 2018940039

Cover design by George Stevens.
Layout design by Megan Elger.

This publication is designed to provide accurate and authoritative information in regard to the subject matter covered. It is sold with the understanding that the publisher is not engaged in rendering legal, accounting, or other professional services. If legal advice or other expert assistance is required, the services of a competent professional person should be sought.

Advantage Media Group is proud to be a part of the Tree Neutral® program. Tree Neutral offsets the number of trees consumed in the production and printing of this book by taking proactive steps such as planting trees in direct proportion to the number of trees used to print books. To learn more about Tree Neutral, please visit **www.treeneutral.com**.

Since 1917, the Forbes mission has remained constant. Global Champions of Entrepreneurial Capitalism. ForbesBooks exists to further that aim by bringing the Stories, Passion, and Knowledge of top thought leaders to the forefront. ForbesBooks brings you The Best in Business. To be considered for publication, please visit **www.forbesbooks.com**.

To the most important cord in my life ... my family.

To my loving parents, Paul and Jeanette; to my beautiful, amazing, and supportive wife, Heather; and to our wonderful children, Ella and Luca, who make their parents proud with each day that passes.

To my clients and team at the office from which I have learned so much: I am so grateful for the opportunity to lead and serve.

To the American entrepreneur who can solve any of the worlds challenges: ever since the first colonists landed in the "The New World," the American entrepreneur has forged ahead in their quest for a better life based on the promise of capitalism and independence.

TABLE OF CONTENTS

THIRD CORD: YOUR FAMILY

HAPPINESS...

Who says money cannot buy happiness?

It certainly can if we stop being workaholics, micromanaging every aspect of business, consistently creating stress for ourselves and our coworkers while having little to no personal or family time. All that chaos leads to a life which was never part of our original plan of why we went into business in the first place.

I've known Rocco Carriero his entire life. Our families, myself included, migrated from southern Italy from a province called Basilicata. I was eleven when we came to this country. There was little to no work in southern Italy. Our greatest natural resources were the people that left those areas to new countries for a better life. As with all immigrants, they typically socialized and supported one another. It became the extended family unit. It has been an honor and truly enlightening to watch Rocco evolve into an amazing person, family man, private wealth advisor—but even more importantly—a great life advisor. I am proud to share my perspective on the *Three Cords Approach* having gone through the process myself.

Marrying a wonderful woman and having three amazing boys at an early age while balancing life and my company was challenging. I started my company, J. Tortorella Swimming Pools, a pool construction and service business in 1981 and we grew at a very rapid pace to become one of America's Top Pool Construction companies based in Southampton, NY. We were profitable, but I was operating under constant stress and making poor investment decisions along the way. I stressed my management team out and I stressed out my family as well. This book, *Three Cords Approach to Life and Wealth Management for Business Owners,* is a wonderful guide to kickoff one's path to happiness in the three most critical areas of a business persons life: their family life, their business/financial life, and themselves as an individual.

It all starts with us. No book will guarantee the results if we resist change, if we are unable recognize our shortfalls or fail to plan. It is said that the definition of insanity is doing the same thing repeatedly and expecting different results. Our happy path needs to be properly planned. I'm considered a visionary and, as with most visionaries, we need to align ourselves with implementers. I surround myself with a team that supports, plans, and helps me implement my vision. This frees up an inordinate amount time to spend with friends, family, and other personal pursuits. Through countless hours of business and personal discussions with Rocco, this book and this process, called the Three Cords Approach, has helped to give me a better perspective on life itself. I was one of Rocco's earliest clients and we have grown together. Prior to practicing Rocco's Three Cords Approach I was operating a fast-paced and unsustainable lifestyle. Building various businesses, always on the go, making investment decisions without much thought other than hoping that the advice of the various people was to my benefit. Many times, it was not. Prior to looking at business and life from the Three Cords perspective, I had no clear investment purpose, did not understand the why's around my investments, had no business continuation plan and no comprehensive financial planning strategy. Prior to practicing

Paul and Jeanette Carriero were immigrants from the south of Italy who worked hard to do their best for me, their only child. They developed in me a sense of independence from an early age. Once, for instance, when I was only twelve years old, they invited me to sit at the kitchen table to join the discussions with a contractor for a renovation and expansion to our house in Patchogue. Together we reviewed the costs and the timelines.

I felt gratified to be invited into the adult world when I was a boy barely out of elementary school. My parents made it clear that they valued my perspective and views. They cared about what I could contribute—and that included helping them to avoid any language and cultural barriers that might lead to misunderstandings. My father was a bright man, but his formal education ended in the fifth grade—and that was in Italy, where both he and my mother had lived well into adulthood.

I know that many of my boyhood classmates got more parental assistance than my mother and father could provide. My parents weren't exactly the best resource in prepping for a vocabulary or grammar quiz, for example. At home they spoke Italian to each other, although they tried to speak to me in English because they were determined that I would learn the language. It was more like a mishmash of Italian and English, but I was able to sort it out to become fluent in both.

I knew that I had to figure things out for myself. In hindsight, that was a blessing. My parents gave me a sense of empowerment and ingenuity. They didn't just give me easy answers—they gave me the incentive to find my own answers. What they did was prepare me for life.

Still, I had some hard lessons to come. My parents valued education and had saved diligently so that I might go to college. And so I did. I headed off to school in Providence, Rhode Island, and proceeded to have the time of my life—just not academically. In my sophomore year at age nineteen, the school politely asked me to go home for focusing more on the fun and not enough on the grades.

It wasn't as if paying for college was a breeze for my parents. They had scraped by so that I might have the opportunity to go to school. They wanted to give me every chance to excel in my new college career. But, in short, that wasn't going to happen. Not yet.

As I look back on that day when I was asked to go home and get my priorities together, I believe it was the best thing that could have happened to me under the circumstances. This was my turning point. I knew I had let my family down and that I had let myself down. Both embarrassed and profoundly convicted, I came to grips with adult responsibility. I was a man, and in the coming years, I would show the world what a man could do. Nobody was going to do this for me. I had to figure it out for myself.

I strongly believe that people should take full responsibility for their lives and not just let things happen to them. They should not accept whatever comes their way. They should set goals and pursue them.

"Things don't just happen; things happen just," wrote Jim Rohn, entrepreneur and motivational author.[1] We create our own outcomes. There are consequences to our actions, and as we look back, we can indeed see the reason that things turned out as they did. It's how we dealt with what we were served. Tough lessons can be some of the best lessons if we grow stronger and move forward, wiser from the experience. We forge and shape our values that way.

A few years back I got together with an old college friend, a graphic artist, to develop a Carriero family crest. I wanted to hang it high so that all could know what we stand for. Its design pays tribute to our Italian American heritage and to my parents' hometown in Italy, and it depicts a needle and thread representing my father's trade as a tailor.

---

1   Jim Rohn, *Leading an Inspired Life*, (Illinois: Nightingale-Conant, 1996).

On the crest are these words: family, helping others, respect, generosity, and personal growth. Those are our cherished values that I wanted to highlight on the crest.

I believe strongly that family must come first. One must always weigh what really matters. I was recently invited to a conference where I could have met former president George W. Bush, the speaker—but the next day was my daughter's tenth birthday. My little

> *I believe strongly that family must come first.*

girl's smiles mattered far more to me. Being there for ball games and practices and putting aside the loads of office work—which I truly enjoy—for a few hours is super important as well. I coach my son Luca's baseball team, and between two practices and two games weekly it takes a lot of time away from the office. Being there and coaching not only Luca but also the other young kids in the community for this short time is priceless and I can never get that time back. Seeing Luca's face after he hit the ball deep into outfield after practicing it over and over for many hours is one of my favorite memories of us together. Being there to watch Luca's growth and development is what it is all about. Being there for those special moments and being present at any and all expense is critical to the family "cord" we talk about in this book.

Most recently I was invited to a friend's birthday golf trip in Spain. The other guys left a few days before me; I couldn't head out with them because that was the week of Ella's sixth-grade graduation. I had planned to leave the evening of her graduation right after the ceremony, assuming the festivities would be over by 8:00 p.m. The ceremony did not end until 8:20 p.m., and that extra twenty minutes of being there for Ella meant me missing my flight to Spain. I had to rebook the flight for following day, eat the cost of a new ticket, miss a round of golf, and still pay for it. Not to mention also still having to pay for a night's stay at an expensive five-star Spanish luxury hotel which I did not even get to sleep at. All of that was part of the deal I made when I chose to stay the extra time at Ella's graduation. Was the extra twenty minutes more of being at the graduation worth the thousands of dollars of extra cost, time lost in Spain, and some added stress? Absolutely. Being there that evening and seeing Ella's full graduation and seeing her receive President Trump's Award for Excellence and Outstanding Achievement in Education was worth every penny and every single minute of being there. When my father took ill, my priority was to make sure he got the best of care. I set everything aside to go with him to his oncologist appointments in the city. I would have spent my last penny on specialists if that could have cured him. I am not sharing this to impress you. My goal is to impress upon you. I just wanted to make the point around being there when we should be there for our family. With family, it should never be about the convenience of our personal time or when it is good for our busy professional life. Its about being there when our family needs us there, no matter the time and no matter the financial cost.

The desire to help others came naturally to me as I grew up in a family where we all pitched in to serve. Our extended family was like a community in which we offered up our various strengths to support one another in our weaknesses. As a boy, I was encouraged to rake the neighbors' leaves. After installing telephone jacks in our house, I found my newfound skills soon put to use in the homes of our relatives and all around the neighborhood. I was pleased to be of service. That spirit of helpfulness, of sharing what I had learned so that others could benefit, became such an indelible part of me that I wanted to incorporate it in our family crest.

Respect, too, is a core value of our family. We must respect others, certainly. It is our duty to be considerate of other people's feelings, treating them the way we would like to be treated, and eager to reciprocate good deeds. I also felt that our family crest should express the importance of generosity. We should give to others, even more than they would expect, and find joy in doing so.

Another of our values is personal growth. Ever since my faltering start in college, I have strived to be the best at whatever I undertake. We must learn, practice, persevere, and, above all, we must dream. If we are not moving forward, we are going backward. If we are not growing, we are dying. Steve Jobs had it right in his Apple marketing campaign: "The people who are crazy enough to think they can change the world are the ones who do."[2] Every year, my family and I set goals and try to do things better than the previous year. We work together to find that right balance between

---

2   Apple Inc., "Think Different" ad campaign (Rob Siltanen, Lee Clow, and Craig Tanimoto, TBWA\Chiat\Day), 1997.

enjoying life and working hard for the future. Each of us seeks to be our very best—happy, healthy, and productive.

And as you read on, you'll find those values from my family crest woven through the pages of this book. They are central to success in one's personal, business, and family life. They are the very fibers of the "three cords" approach to life that we will examine—with a particular emphasis on family business planning. I have built my own financial advisory business from the ground up, and therefore I understand the dreams and the struggles of family businesses. I have worked with numerous businesspeople who have created impressive wealth, starting at zero. Through education and experience, in my field and in life itself, I know what it takes to attain success, and I wish to help others along that path.

By living life purposefully with a sense of determination, you can attain the success of your dreams. It is my privilege to be your guide in your search for the best of the best.

Whether you are striving to build your fortune or are ready to transition your life's work and make the most of the proceeds, you can advance confidently with every step. By living life purposefully with a sense of determination, you can attain the success of your dreams. It is my privilege to be your

guide in your search for the best of the best.

INTRODUCTION
THE PERFECT FIT

---

*The biggest mistake people make in life is not trying
to make a living at doing what they most enjoy.*
—MALCOLM FORBES

My father was a tailor, and though he didn't want me to become one, too—he wanted me to get an education—I became one nonetheless. I am a "tailor" of customized financial plans.

At the shop that he operated in our Long Island town, my father put in seven-day weeks to provide for his family. He had learned the trade at a young age in Italy, where he grew up in the Basilicata region in the town of Montescaglioso. His father died when he was a baby, and he and his siblings were sent to work while still children. One of his sisters became a teacher, the other a seamstress, and his brother eventually opened a stationery store. It was decided that my father would apprentice in his uncle's tailor shop.

After he married, he and my mother decided to emigrate to America. Much of her family had already come here, and she yearned to be with them—and so in 1962 they relocated to Long Island, where my father went to work for a local tailor in Patchogue. He saved his money, and after a decade or so, about the time that I was born, he was able to purchase the shop.

As a boy, I often would hang around that shop, but my father didn't want me to learn to use the machinery. He told me he wanted a better path for me. And so I watched. As he went about his business, I observed him, as well as the previous owner who still helped him out. I saw my father put together ensembles in which all the pieces must work together on many levels. He listened carefully to his customers' needs, and he came up with solutions. He tweaked the fit to meet their requirements.

What he demonstrated to me was that running a business calls for daily dedication. My father often would stay late or go in early to finish an alteration for a loyal customer who needed a suit to be finished sooner than usual for a special occasion. Even on Sundays, he would stop in at the shop in the morning to check on things. I saw firsthand what customer service was all about.

The men and women who patronized his shop would share stories with him, and he would listen intently. He cared about them and their families. If a customer passed away, he would pay his respects at the wake. A lot of politicians came to the shop to have their suits done, but he didn't much share his political views—except to say that any candidate who was one of his customers stood a good chance of getting his vote.

My father knew that growing a business meant developing good relationships. He knew that by treating his customers right, by going above and beyond to serve them, they would come back again and again. He strived to be the best at what he did. He would always give people more than what they paid for.

To this day, I think of him as I attend to the needs and wishes of my own clients. As I tailor their financial plans, I design for the perfect fit—measuring, trimming, balancing—trying to go above and beyond. I get to know each of my clients so that I understand what they need and why. I do alterations to specification so that they will have the right style for the right season. And I hope my father—rest his soul—knows that he taught me well.

THE STRONGEST CORD

As masters of fabric and thread, tailors understand the principle of the "triple-braided cord." It's the wisdom of Solomon: Such a rope is not easily broken. It makes the best lifeline.

I have arranged the sections of this book to represent those three cords as they apply to the men and women who operate businesses that make things and offer services in communities far and wide. Many of my clients operate such businesses, and each of them, in his or her own way, is weaving together three essential cords. Whether you operate a business or not, I am sure that you will recognize how each of them contributes to a strong and productive life.

Yourself

The first is the cord of "yourself"—your personal growth and development. Where are you going in life? What are your goals? As you hurry about taking care of this or that, have you paused long enough to consider why you do what you do? Do you take time off from your professional pursuits to get in touch with yourself? Are you taking care of your health, both physical and emotional? Do you let yourself dream? What are your hobbies?

You will find greater strength when you find the appropriate balance between life and work.

Your business

The second is the cord of "your business." What has been your purpose in nurturing it along? What has been your vision and mission? Do you intend to pass it on to your children, if any of them are interested? Or do you plan to sell it to a key employee, perhaps, or an outside buyer? In other words: What is your exit strategy? How can you negotiate to get the best price with the greatest tax efficiency for all concerned? And as you build your business, how can you best position yourself and your family for a more secure future? To what extent, and in what ways, have you invested outside your business as well as in it? Have you considered and dealt with all the many risks to your financial security that you could face? You spent years growing your business to maturity. Now, you need to invest for success for the many years still to come.

Your family

The third is the cord of "your family." How is your home life? Are you satisfied with the quality of your relationships with loved ones? Have you found fulfillment in the time and experiences that you have shared? Once you have retired, what do you plan to do with that pile of money that represents your life's work? How will you transition it into a reliable income that maintains the lifestyle to which you and your family have been accustomed? What arrangements have you made to cope with the inevitability that your body and mind will grow old and frail? If you or your spouse should need long-term care, how will you pay for that without sacrificing the needs and wants of your family? The cord of family involves making sure that you have dealt with all the nuts and bolts of estate planning, but it also involves legacy planning: What do you want to pass on to future generations besides the money and the "stuff"? What do you want them to understand about your values and what mattered most to you during your time on earth? Will they think only of your worldly goods, or will they think of the good you have done for the world?

As you weave together each of those cords of your life, you may find that one or another of them has grown frayed.

Some people, as the years have passed, find that they have placed so much emphasis on business that their family life has suffered, or that they no longer feel a sense of self, or that incessant stress has wrecked their health. Other people launch a promising enterprise only to see it fade for lack of attention as they pursue their personal interests. Still others find the responsibilities of family so overwhelming that they forget what it was like to dream.

When all three of those cords are tightly braided, the result is a bigger, better, stronger cord. Unless you are strong in all those areas, something is likely to snap. You may be doing very well in one of those areas, while elsewhere you feel as if you are at the breaking point. We have all heard stories of the hard-driving business owner

> *When all three of those cords are tightly braided, the result is a bigger, better, stronger cord.*

who overindulges in food or booze and whose idea of exercise is a ride in a golf cart—and dies of a heart attack. Or the one who joins all the clubs and associations and serves on several boards while finding time to work out regularly at the gym but spends virtually no time with family. Or the one so devoted to family that the business gets short shrift.

Such scenarios are far from unusual. To lead a balanced life, in which the triple-braided cord is strong, is not easy. It doesn't just happen. It calls for concerted effort and careful planning. Each cord depends on the others, and so none must be neglected. If your family life gets out of control, you may be unable to focus on your business, and if your business fails, you may feel that you have lost a big part of your identity and cease to take care of yourself. Any weakness in the braid results in far more stress on the rest of it.

> *To lead a balanced life, in which the triple-braided cord is strong, is not easy. It doesn't just happen. It calls for concerted effort and careful planning. Each cord depends on the others, and so none must be neglected.*

It's not that any one of the three is more important than the others. All three matter. All three need to be maintained—not necessarily with equal attention at any given time, but with full consideration at all times. Yes, you may need to focus on business at times, but you must not throw yourself into your work to the point where little else matters. Yes, you deserve to spend time on your own interests and hobbies, but not to the point where you are self-centered and oblivious to the needs of others. Much of this is a matter of maturity. Life has a way of teaching the importance of keeping the cord strong.

Finding the right balance can be particularly difficult for the businessperson. To succeed in business, you must be a good leader, and good leaders must exhibit this trinity of strength. And yet for many, the business is paramount. Personal and family considerations pale in comparison. In fact, businesspeople often have trouble envisioning what life will be like after they move on from the business, as they one day surely must do in one way or another. The business has long been the source of their identity. They have not stopped to consider how they will feel once they are separated from what they have done for thirty-plus years. They are the business, and the business is them—and once they say goodbye, then what?

Some have had enough and are eager to end all those years of hard work. Others are far more ambivalent. They may find the transition into retirement to be more stressful than relaxing. What helps to reduce that stress is to start planning early, and not just the financial details. Money does matter, and handling it well is an important attribute of the three cords. You will be reading a lot about that in this book. However, you must also attend to the non-financial matters. What will you do with all that wealth that you spend so many years building? What will make life meaningful to you? Strengthening the cord really amounts to finding life balance.

You will notice that in the three-section structure of this book, the cord of family comes last. That does not imply that it is the least important. A good family life is the culmination of developing a good personal and business life. It starts with understanding yourself, the first cord. What fulfills you? What are your goals, your dreams? If you never find yourself, you really cannot be of much help to other people. Once you help yourself, you are in a far better position to be of service to others. You will gain the energy and initiative to run a business, providing something that is valuable to others. And as you succeed there, you will be building the resources to give your loved ones the very best. Because they came first, they were your endgame all along.

DOING IT RIGHT

Some of my clients are first-generation millionaires, in their fifties or older, who started out with basically nothing and accumulated wealth through their business pursuits. Many of them are centered in the New York metropolitan region and have built multimillion-dollar enterprises from zero. They operate, or have operated, a wide range of enterprises, from construction and service-based companies to doctor/medical service practices and manufacturing businesses.

By and large, they are people who work hard every day and who build and produce things as well as help to take care of and fix people. I do work with corporate executives, and a percentage of my clients are the surviving spouses in businesses where the owners have passed on. I continue to serve those families, providing the level of care to which they have long been accustomed.

A typical client may have liquid investment assets of $5million-plus, and many of them have businesses that gross at least $5 million. I have had clients with a net worth of $50 million to $100 million, and I've also worked with people with investable assets of $1 million. These are not extravagant people, for the most part. They tend to live simply. They are the "millionaire next door" type. Having "made it," they now want to do something besides make more. They want to do it right.

These are folks who care deeply about their families and about their legacy. They think about the footprint that they will leave after they are gone. To that end, they are seeking good advice and good service. They are the kind of people who expect you to be there for them when they need you. You must earn their trust by proving yourself to be reliable, consistent, and caring.

Most of them are at the point in their lives where they are looking to do much more than build wealth. They care about investing wisely, of course, but they know that means more than getting the highest return possible, whatever the risks might be.

They know true wealth requires more than comparing performances and beating some benchmark.

The *Three Cords Approach* is therefore not a book of specific investment advice. This is not a book for people who care only about where they might position their money so that they might amplify their net worth from, say, $30 million to $100 million. Such growth is important, of course, and we do focus on it. However, a family's circumstances, goals, and needs will determine the best way to manage their money. The intent must govern the investments.

That is why you must get to know your advisor. In this book, we will look at a variety of investment vehicles that are used for appropriate purposes, but I can make no recommendations without getting to know the individual and the requirements of the business and the family. Only then can I determine what would be the right fit.

> *This book, then, is for families who want to put together a comprehensive plan that covers their financial lives and much more.*

It is not all about the rate of return. If I were to focus solely on that but failed to help people achieve their personal goals or accomplish their family planning, did it really matter in the end? Nothing is wrong, of course, with setting financial objectives. Any business owner would like the idea of multiplying his or her net worth—but it must be done the right way, incorporating all three of the cords for the greatest strength. It must be done in the context of what ultimately is best for the individual, the business, and the family.

This book, then, is for families who want to put together a comprehensive plan that covers their financial lives and much more. They care about where they have been in life and where they are going, and they are looking for help as they take the next steps on their journey. They are looking for balance in their personal, business, and family lives. In doing so, they see the importance of clarifying their purposes and setting tangible goals.

This book is for those who want to make a difference in the world, who are concerned about the direction that their loved ones are taking and about the values that they embrace, who want to leave a legacy, whether to family or charity, in dollars or deeds.

> *This book is for those who want to make a difference in the world, who are concerned about the direction that their loved ones are taking and about the values that they embrace, who want to leave a legacy, whether to family or charity, in dollars or deeds.*

In these pages, I am speaking to those who want to make the most of the business that they have nurtured. They want to grow it to its best and then either sell it to an eager buyer or transition it within the family, and they want to know the most efficient way to do so.

This book is for you if you would like to learn tested-in-the-trenches strategies from a financial advisor who has helped many successful people customize and coordinate the diverse elements of retirement planning. In short, if you are looking for a good tailor, read on.

Paul Carriero's shop in Patchogue, NY

Paul Carriero at work in the shop

Paul Carriero with Rocco's children, Luca and Ella

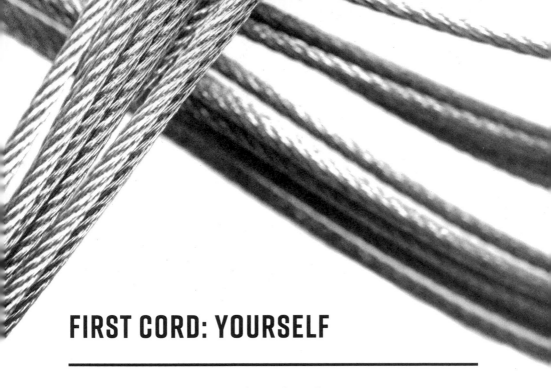

FIRST CORD: YOURSELF

*Too many people overvalue what they are
not and undervalue what they are.*

—**MALCOLM FORBES**

After my first unsuccessful attempt at my undergraduate degree because of having too much fun, my father thought I may need to do something else besides college. He loved and accepted me, but I had to do something—and he had a friend who might be able to get me a job at his packing plant. He figured that maybe I just wasn't college material; I had tried that route, and the college had sent me shuffling home. At that point, he just wanted me to get a real job.

I had other ideas. I deeply felt the humiliation of failure, and adding to my distress was that few people knew the real reason for my abridged college career—that I had been more interested in partying than studying. Many of my relatives, like my father, also concluded that I may not be cut out for the academic life and that I should close the book on that chapter and move on.

I did move on. I had been aiming toward an undergraduate degree in communications and advertising, and so instead of taking the shipping plant job, I resolved to get a real-life position in the business that was supposed to have been my field of study. Leafing through a local "help wanted" flyer, I saw an opening to sell ads for a magazine featuring homes for sale by owner.

It was a terrific experience. It was my foot in the door to advertising and marketing and sales. At such a small company, I worked directly with the owner. I earned enough to enroll in community college with the mission of getting my associate degree. That was part of my master plan to prove to myself and to the world that I could excel in college. It was a two-year program that I completed in one, taking twenty-four credits per semester and getting all As and Bs. I then enrolled once again at Johnson and Wales University in Providence, from where I had come home in chagrin just a few years earlier, and finally earned my undergraduate degree in communications and advertising.

During college, I had my first experience in the financial services world, in which I had developed an interest. My girlfriend, Heather—who would later become my wife—was the nanny for the family of a financial advisor, who hired me as an intern. While I was there, a magazine article portrayed him unfairly as a rude, cigar-chomping sort, and he had told the reporter some things off the record that got into print. The brokerage firm fired him. I knew the man, and he was not what the article made him out to be. The experience gave me a bad impression of how things worked in corporate America, particularly in financial services.

After graduating, I returned to work at that real estate publishing firm—and then decided to get my master's degree. Despite that unsettling experience during my internship, I pursued a degree in banking and finance. I wanted to get back into that business and do things right.

And so, at an early age, after facing down the prospect of failure, I took charge of my life—and I haven't looked back. It was the beginning of a journey of self-growth and development. What finally had motivated me was the desire to prove myself as good at something. I learned the power of setting distinct goals with the determination to reach them, step by step.

I learned, in other words, the power of having a strong sense of "yourself"—and that, as we will explore in this section, is the first element of a strong, three-cord approach. If you develop that one first, all else will follow. Unless you have a confident sense of self, unless you are in touch with your goals and dreams and feel the motivation to go after them, how can you expect to operate a business involving service to others? How can you expect to take good care of your family?

I learned, in other words, the power of having a strong sense of "yourself"—and that, as we will explore in this section, is the first element of a strong, three-cord approach. If you develop that one first, all else will follow. Unless you have a confident sense of self, unless you are in touch with your goals and dreams and feel the motivation to go after them, how can you expect to operate a business involving service to others? How can you expect to take good care of your family?

Visionary leadership is firmly rooted in self-awareness. "Know thyself," the classical Greek philosophers urged, and everything in moderation. That is how you begin to make things happen.

CHAPTER 1
WHAT'S NEXT IN LIFE?

Success follows doing what you want to do.
There is no other way to be successful.

—MALCOLM FORBES

"If you don't fly first class, your kids someday certainly will," I have often told couples as we begin to forge the details of a financial plan. Those are the couples who have succeeded. They are the ones whom I am pleased to inform, after a careful review, that they could be spending considerably more than they had thought was appropriate.

Unfortunately, I have had to tell other couples that they cannot continue their high-flying lifestyle if they expect their resources to last for as many years as their bodies will. They are on course to run out of money before they run out of life.

Why do people pinch pennies when they do not need to do so? Why do they hold back on fulfilling their goals and dreams, or even hesitate to have a little fun, in retirement? It's because they just don't know. They have not thought through what the future might hold for them, and they are running scared, even if they have a net worth in the millions. Some people are naturally frugal—perhaps they were raised that way, or something in their marrow makes them loathe to spend, which could well have contributed to an impressive growth in their portfolio. Or they might be harking back to a time when money was scarce for them. It's sad, though, when they are missing out on so much that they could do. They are sacrificing memories.

And it is just as sad to see couples blow through their savings early in retirement because they, too, really don't have a clue about what they can afford to do. I have seen people withdrawing 10 percent a year from their investment accounts when 3 percent should be their limit. I'm not saying that they are spendthrifts, necessarily. They may have lofty goals and even a spirit of benefi-

> *Perhaps the biggest risk that people face in life is not knowing.*

cence that leads them to want to help out everybody who asks—but they just don't have the dollars to do it all. Perhaps they have retired from successful businesses and careers and figure this is finally their time to let loose. What they really need to do is get a grip, before it's too late.

Perhaps the biggest risk that people face in life is not knowing. They haven't gained a clear picture of where they are going, and so they live day by day, doing this or that and spending along the way, in whatever amount seems right at the time. They are rambling along with no real vision for what they might accomplish. Without clear goals, without a comprehensive plan for life, they can easily lapse into overspending or underspending.

A great financial advisor's job is to help people think it through so that they make it to the destination of their choosing. And by that, I don't mean reaching some arbitrary sum that they would like to see in their accounts. You should not simply be aiming for some magic number, but rather for the number that makes sense for you and that will help you

> *Without clear goals, without a comprehensive plan for life, they can easily lapse into overspending or underspending.*

bring meaning to your life. I help people set aside the dollars for their dreams.

So much depends on the situation and the family dynamics. I have met couples who have plenty of resources, but husband and wife just don't seem to get along or want to do much together. It's a sad truth. I have met other couples who feel like newlyweds and yet one or the other lacks the physical health to do the things they had dreamed about. Others are happy together and healthy, but their children, though grown, are troubled. They feel they need to stay nearby to help them out. All those situations can get in the way. The good news is that I see plenty of happy couples in good health with plenty of resources and nothing holding them back. It's time to enjoy life.

You can enjoy life, of course, under a wide variety of circumstances. It's a matter of perspective. You need to know yourself, and you need to know your limits. You shouldn't go beyond them, but neither should you fall short of them. Your financial advisor should help you find those boundaries, and I encourage you to do the best with what you have. The financial advisor's goal is to help people do things right.

I have found, in working with numerous people through the years, that those most willing to talk about the big picture are the ones who do the best. They are interested in discussing much more than investments and rates of return and benchmarks, as important as those are. They want to talk about goals and objectives and the legacy they will leave, financial and otherwise. They are as interested in defining their values as they are in counting their valuables.

Success comes best to those who strive to figure out how all the pieces to comprehensive financial planning should fall into place. Those are the ones who manage to make sense of it all, and in doing so they gain a true perspective on the meaning of money.

PONDERING YOUR PURPOSE

As people get older and their business careers mature, they find themselves increasingly confronting a fundamental and soul-searching question: What's it all about? What has been the point of their life's work? To what purpose? If they are not asking themselves the question, it is high time that they do—and those who become my clients will find that we talk about such matters early in our rela-

> *Success comes best to those who strive to figure out how all the pieces to comprehensive financial planning should fall into place. Those are the ones who manage to make sense of it all, and in doing so they gain a true perspective on the meaning of money.*

tionship. I need to know, too. Their answers will be central to the decisions we will be making together on a wide range of issues.

Many people presume that we will jump right into the investments, and they often come to the initial meeting with an armful of statements and documents, ready to roll. And that's good—we will be needing that information, just not immediately. First things first, and that means getting to know each other. Effective planning and wealth management must be predicated on a relationship of trust that only just get started with a handshake.

> *Effective planning and wealth management must be predicated on a relationship of trust that only just get started with a handshake.*

Doing more advanced forms of financial planning encompasses so much more than how to make the best plays with your money. Yes, your investments are highly important, and wealth management will be much of what we talk about as we build our relationship. But we will also explore the broader topics of tax planning and the many types of risk that must be addressed if you are to have a more secure financial future. We will put our heads together to develop an exit strategy for your business that works well for all involved. We will examine effective and efficient ways to plan for passing on your estate and a legacy for your loved ones and the world.

In the chapters ahead, we will look at the aspects of a more advanced and comprehensive plan, and more. First, though, it's time to lay the groundwork. What is your *why*? Where are you going? Do you know how to get there? What's the best way to travel? Your money is there to serve you on your journey. How, then, do you wish to be served?

> *What is your why? Where are you going? Do you know how to get there? What's the best way to travel? Your money is there to serve you on your journey. How, then, do you wish to be served?*

It's time to organize, prioritize, and crystallize your dreams. As a couple, write down your objectives. Who and what is important to you? What makes you feel happy and fulfilled? What goals do you wish to develop together, and individually? Where would you like to travel? Do you desire to launch another career, or business, or pursue an education? Do you have a hobby that brings you pleasure? Is there anyone, or any charity, that you want to support, either with your dollars or with your time? In other words: What do you plan to do with your money, and what do you hope to accomplish? How would you like to be remembered?

THE MEANING OF MONEY

Early in our relationship, I ask a series of questions to develop a profile of people with whom I will be working. I ask them what they value most in life, and what they ultimately want to achieve. I ask about their vision for the future.

One of those key questions is this: "What is important to you about money?" It's a question that gets to the bottom of their motivations. It tells me how they feel about the importance of accumulating assets and of preserving them. Nobody has ever responded, "Well, I just want stacks and stacks of money all the way to the ceiling!" They usually see some purpose, some meaning, something that the money represents to them, something that it can do that is central to their values.

For example, I often get responses similar to this: "Money is important because we don't want to become dependent on our children." It is one way of saying that they value their financial independence and don't want to be relying on others. That's the most common response to that question, and it highlights a fundamental desire for dignity and freedom of choice. In fact, the word *freedom* comes up frequently. People say they want the freedom to do what they want, when they want. Again: it's about independence and self-reliance. They fear losing that, and they see money as the means to preserve it.

Though people often mention their charitable intentions and the mark they wish to leave on the world, that is seldom the initial focus. It is important to them, but they don't start there. Their first thoughts often turn to family. That's where they want to leave a legacy. They want to provide something for their family.

As we uncover their goals and objectives, couples have often told me that they are concerned about their assets remaining within the family bloodline. They want their money, or their business, to pass to their children, and then to their grandchildren. They are looking for a way to make sure it doesn't get into the hands of a son-in-law, or daughter-in-law, and find its way out of the immediate family. They may perceive their children's marriages as less than solid, to the point where their legacy could be lost in a divorce settlement. It's a sign of our times.

At this early stage in the planning, those profile questions help to guide both me and the client. I find out what matters to them, what motivates them. Often, they are learning those things for the first time, as well. They are gaining clarity—and that, essentially, is what people are looking for when they seek financial planning advice. They are looking for direction, and they hope to move forward with confidence that they have made the right choices.

As we work together, an early step is to make sure their goals and objectives are realistic and that their available resources can support them. Many of my clients come to me with substantial savings, and so that generally is the case—although their dreams can be outsize, too. It takes a prodigious portfolio, for example, to support several residences. For the most part, however, we can align the resources with the goals. That's the clarity that builds the confidence.

The job of a financial advisor or wealth manager is to help people see the possibilities and get the right perspective on what they can accomplish. I can help them take wing, but sometimes I need to help keep them down to earth.

A CHALLENGING STAGE OF LIFE

As you plan for the years ahead, you are preparing for a major transition in life. One day you will be moving from the mind-set of accumulating to the mind-set of making good use of what you have accumulated. That alone requires a new way of thinking—but it's more than that.

Retirement will be a time of redefining your identity. You no doubt are familiar with that feeling of coming to grips with who you really are. It happened in adolescence. It happened, perhaps, when you launched your business, when you married, when you had children, when you became a homeowner. Those times of change can be exciting. They can also be troubling—and retirement is no exception.

The time will come when you wake up on a Monday morning with no need to get up, get showered, and get out the door. You are no longer the one at the helm of the business that you nurtured along for decades. The people you left behind at the workplace are looking to someone else for leadership. How will you feel? What will you do with the hours in your day? Many people give little thought to what this transition will be like. Perhaps they imagined a cruise or two, or strolls on the beach, or blissful days relaxing at home on the sunporch—but then what?

Not only do you need to find a way to replace your income in retirement, you also must find the new you. This is a matter for both spouses to consider carefully. The transition to a new stage of life can rock a marriage, particularly when lingering issues have gone unresolved. The togetherness that results from being around the house all day is not necessarily all that pleasant. Strengthening that union is important not just for your emotional well-being, but also for your financial well-being. Divorce is increasingly common during retirement, and it can devastate the heart. It also can devastate the asset side of the balance sheet.

That is what can be at stake if you retire without a purpose to replace the workplace. Life can get boring, even depressing. The good news is that you can do so much to anticipate this change of life. Advance planning, done properly, needs to examine the many ways in which you can continue to feel connected. How can you remain productive? How can you feel that you are still contributing?

Some people allow themselves a slower transition into retirement. They keep a hand in their business, or in their profession, working as consultants or mentoring younger people. Some decide to put their energies into another business, perhaps one that they have dreamed about for many years but lacked the time to pursue. Others devote their hours to volunteer work for charities and causes that they find meaningful. Some go back to school—not necessarily to develop a new career, but for the sheer satisfaction of learning.

I have seen many business owners sell their businesses thinking they may regret the decision because this is all they have known for the past thirty-plus years, but most don't feel this way. After I asked one of my clients if he wished he would have sold his business sooner, he said, "Yes, I wish I had done it sooner because of how much I am enjoying life now and how free I have become." He also shared that his "biggest lesson [after selling] has been that after you have all you need with material items and have enough resources to sustain the lifestyle you would like for the rest of your life, any more time running the business and dealing with the stresses that come with it is just wasting your life's time, and the sooner you are able to realize that the sooner you will be on your path to true wealth and happiness."

This can be a time of intense personal development. Many people find themselves busier, and happier, than ever as they embark on some of life's finest years. The key is to begin planning early and anticipating this new chapter. You should not just let retirement happen to you by default. It should be done by design. A great financial advisor has seen what works and what doesn't work. I have seen what works, and what doesn't work. You need the right financial advisor who will help you to do it right.

NEW WORLD OF CONCERNS

Think back to your younger years. What occupied your thoughts then? If you were like so many people, you saved to buy a house and anticipated raising a family—but wondered how you could ever afford it, particularly if one of you had to give up a salary to take care of the children. Somehow you managed, even if it meant taking on debt. You worked hard to develop your business or to improve your family's lifestyle. And then you started thinking about the cost of your children's college education. There seemed to be too little of you to go around. You wondered how you would ever have time to do it all.

From another perspective, though, time seemed endless as you looked at the years ahead. At the pace you were going, it was hard to imagine yourself as retired someday. Nonetheless, you dutifully began setting aside funds for that far-off day, taking advantage of the 401(k) plans or IRAs. Your contributions added up, month after month, flowing automatically into a couple of mutual funds that you chose at the outset. The market's fluctuations didn't overly concern you then. You figured you wouldn't be touching that money for years, so you had time on your side. If the market sank, it surely would be rising again.

Now, thirty or forty years later, you have a new basket of concerns. The children are grown, you have paid off the mortgage, and as you look at the value of your business or other assets you have accumulated during your career, you wonder whether it's enough to see you through for, perhaps, another thirty or forty years. It is likely that you worry more, now, that the markets could deliver a blow to your holdings. Will the Dow take another dive? Will property prices plunge? You get the feeling that time no longer is on your side. You feel more protective of your investments, less willing to expose them to risk.

In fact, you are more aware—or should be—of an array of threats to your portfolio. What about medical costs and the risk of needing long-term care? How will you deal with income and estate taxes? Inflation? A change in interest rates? How will you pay for those emergencies and contingencies that come to every life? Will you be able to help your children and the grandchildren if they need you?

You feel that you should be safeguarding your money, but at the same time you feel you should be growing it sufficiently to address such challenges. You need a strategy to accomplish both. The way you handled money during your accumulation years could backfire on you now. You need to manage risk by putting a greater emphasis on preservation, but without stifling the growth necessary to maintain your lifestyle.

It's a new world of worries. Retirement is no longer just a concept. You are at its doorstep. Somehow, the distant future turned into the here and now. To be unsure where you stand financially is distressing. This is no time to guess. You need to know. You don't want to scrimp, and you don't want to splurge. You need to get it just right—and you do so by first setting your sights on a clear vision for your life, and then working out the steps that will get you there. That's how you will know when you have arrived.

Rest assured that you are not the first to have faced these matters. I have heard them voiced in my office many times. These are the common themes of life, financial and otherwise, as people prepare for this new adventure. Yes, your circumstances are unique, and so are your goals. You and your family will face your own set of troubles and triumphs. You are one of a kind, but you are not alone. Having worked with so many people facing issues similar to yours, I can help to guide you on the path more likely to bring you the success of your dreams.

WHAT YOU NEED TO KNOW

➡ As you anticipate retiring, you must develop a clear picture of your goals and priorities so that you can move forward confidently, knowing that you are neither underspending nor overspending.

➡ Retirement can be challenging financially, socially, and emotionally. This is a major change of life. Through advance planning, you can deal with those changes appropriately.

➡ Once you have established a life purpose for your retirement, it is time to work out the steps you must take to reach that destination.

CHAPTER 2
TO YOUR HEALTH

A healthy person has a thousand wishes,
but a sick person has only one.

—INDIAN PROVERB

We were watching a soccer game together, my father and I, when he turned to me. "OK … take me back to bed," he said softly. His spine was aching from the cancer that had spread from his lungs. I eased him out of his chair in the house where he and my mother had raised me, working so hard to give me their best. Holding him under his arm tightly, I led him to his bedroom, and as we passed a mirror, he gazed at the image of his son helping him one last time. I stayed with him as he slept and as he slipped into a coma. My father never awoke again.

I had taken him weekly into the city to see an oncologist after his diagnosis. A regimen of therapies, from chemotherapy to meditation, added nearly a year of hopeful and comfortable months to his life. We spent many hours together, sharing our hearts and dreams—but his decades of smoking could not be undone. Just a few days before he passed, I had to tell him: the doctors could do no more, and now it was in God's hands.

Until the cancer gripped him, I cannot recall that this strong family man had ever been sick. But neither do I recall him ever visiting a doctor until then. This was a wake-up call for me. Though I am not a smoker and I enjoy good health, I understand that I must actively take care of my body. I see nutritionists and wellness doctors. I try to exercise. I know my body's numbers. Heart disease and stroke are in my family, and so I get regular checkups from Dr. Wolk, a top cardiologist in New York. In fact, I go to those checkups each year with one of my clients and closest friends. We both are involved in the American Heart Association. One must not ignore health issues that close relatives have experienced.

We must do all we can to promote a long and robust life. I look to the example of my mother, who remains strong and active by virtue of her prudent health habits and regular consultation with doctors. Taking care of yourself is fundamental to planning a fruitful life. If you are not around, what was the point of all that money that you accumulated? What did all those years of hard work avail you?

We must do whatever is in our power to prevent poor health from abridging our dreams. In the Three Cords Approach, don't let the cord of "yourself" be severed. Your business and family aspirations depend on your enduring strength—and yet so often, people neglect their health needs as they pursue business and family priorities.

Taking care of yourself is fundamental to planning a fruitful life. If you are not around, what was the point of all that money that you accumulated? What did all those years of hard work avail you?

Life is fragile. I have known people who were on the verge of enjoying what they had worked so hard to attain—and who then became utterly unable to do so. One gentleman had invested and saved throughout his career, but whenever I assured him he could retire, he always chose to wait one more year, just one more year. And then, visiting his daughter in Paris, he was rushed to the hospital. He died five weeks later of leukemia. I encouraged his wife to get out and enjoy life with the resources they had acquired together, and she did. She managed to do many of the things she had long wanted to do.

I certainly understand how people can be blindsided by such health crises. Sometimes, as with so much else in comprehensive planning, we simply need to take action to increase the chances of success. We should not live in fear of things we cannot control—but we need the wisdom to make whatever changes will enhance the quality of our lives.

Your physical condition, however, is only one aspect of good health. You must attend to your mental and emotional health, as well, and to the quality of your relationships.

Your physical condition, however, is only one aspect of good health. You must attend to your mental and emotional health, as well, and to the quality of your relationships. Stress, for example, is a known killer. The workings of body, mind, and heart are inter-related. One influences the others, and you need to find the right balance that will allow you to live abundantly.

EATING RIGHT

Good nutrition plays a key role in physical well-being. Along with exercise, eating right keeps you at a healthy weight and reduces the risk of heart disease, high blood pressure, type 2 diabetes, osteoporosis, cancer, and other ailments.

About a third of US adults and 17 percent of children and adolescents ages two to nineteen are obese, according to the President's Council on Fitness, Sports, and Nutrition. Teaching young children to eat right will help to instill in them good dietary habits for a lifetime.

Here are some of the healthy eating tips that the council suggests:

- Make half your plate fruits and vegetables.
- Make half the grains you eat whole grains.
- Switch to fat-free or low-fat (1 percent) milk.
- Choose a variety of lean protein foods.
- Compare sodium in foods.
- Drink water instead of sugary drinks.
- Eat some seafood.
- Cut back on solid fats.

EXERCISING REGULARLY

It takes discipline and nobody is perfect, but regular physical activity has been shown time and again to produce significant health benefits. Exercise tones up the body, results in a better night's sleep, and can reduce the risk of chronic illness such as heart disease and cancer, according to the President's Council on Fitness, Sports, and Nutrition (PCFSN).[3] Because it is essential to promoting good health, regular exercise should be part of people's lifestyle from childhood into the retirement years.

Childhood obesity has resulted in an increased incidence of type 2 diabetes at younger ages, according to the PCFSN. Seventy percent of obese teenagers tend to become obese adults. Unless this trend is addressed, the council says, a third of all children born after the year 2000 may become diabetic, and many others will suffer from heart disease, high blood pressure, cancer, and asthma—conditions that are likely to worsen with age.[4]

Regular physical activity, however, has been shown to reduce the three leading health-related causes of death: heart disease, cancer, and stroke. It promotes stronger bone, muscle, and joint development, and improves heart and lung function. Active people tend to sleep better, have better physical stamina, and are less likely

---

3   President's Council on Fitness, Sports and Nutrition, "Importance of Physical Activity," last modified January 26, 2017, https://www.hhs.gov/fitness/be-active/importance-of-physical-activity/index.html.

4   Ibid.

to experience depression. It makes sense: exercise has long been known as a great stress reducer.

A GOOD NIGHT'S SLEEP

At any age, getting sufficient sleep of good quality is essential to good health—both mental and physical. When you are chronically tired, you cannot be at the peak of your productivity and it is hard to enjoy the opportunities that await you in retirement. Children in particular need plenty of sleep if their bodies and brains are to develop properly, according to the National Heart, Lung, and Blood Institute (NHLBI).[5]

Lack of sleep can be a matter of life and death: you cannot safely operate a vehicle or other equipment unless you are well rested and alert. Sleeplessness reduces reaction times and inhibits effective learning and problem solving. The NHLBI points out that it has also been tied to an increased risk of obesity, heart disease, kidney disease, diabetes, and stroke. Insufficient sleep can disrupt the immune system, as well.

A good night's rest can do wonders for your emotional well-being and the quality of your relationships. It's not just that you feel

---

5   *"Your Guide to Healthy Sleep,"* National Heart, Lung, and Blood Institute, 2011, https://www.nhlbi.nih.gov/files/docs/public/sleep/healthy_sleep.pdf.

cranky: sleep deficiency has been shown to be a factor in depression, suicide, and risky behaviors.

DANGERS OF SMOKING

The top cause of preventable disease and death worldwide, according to the American Lung Association, is cigarette smoking.[6] Every year, more than 480,000 Americans die from smoking-related diseases. The estimated societal cost is $150 billion each year in lost productivity and $130 billion a year directly in health care expenditures. That's a cost of about $7,000 for every adult smoker.[7]

Smoking is the cause of about 90 percent of lung cancer deaths and about 80 percent of deaths from chronic obstructive pulmonary diseases such as emphysema and bronchitis, the lung association reports. The habit has been shown to harm nearly every organ in the body. It leads to coronary heart disease, stroke, and many other cancers and diseases. Nonetheless, recent statistics indicate that nearly 18 percent of adults age eighteen and older are

---

6   "Health Effects of Smoking," American Lung Association, accessed August 3, 2017, http://www.lung.org/stop-smoking/smoking-facts/health-effects-of-smoking.html.

7   "The Health Consequences of Smoking—50 Years of Progress: A Report of the Surgeon General," U.S. Department of Health and Human Services, 2014, http://www.surgeongeneral.gov/library/reports/50-years-of-progress/exec-summary.pdf.

still puffing away, and nearly a tenth of high school students are reported to be smokers.

The lung association suggests that counseling and FDA-approved smoking cessation medications, particularly in combination, have proven to be effective in helping people kick the habit. A recent survey found that nearly half of adult smokers had tried to quit in the previous year.[8] With the right help, they can succeed, doing a big favor not only to their own health but to society as well.

REGULAR CHECKUPS

Regular physical exams and screenings can identify health problems before they start or have advanced very far, increasing dramatically the chances for a cure. Given the benefits, you should not consider preventive checkups to be optional. They will significantly increase your chances of a longer and healthier life.

I believe it is essential that you develop an ongoing relationship with a doctor you trust, who feels to you like a good fit. Don't automatically rule out a doctor simply because his or her services are not covered by your insurance policy. You may find that the out-of-pocket expense is less than you imagined. Many doctors

---

8 Ahmed Jamal et al., "Current Cigarette Smoking Among Adults—United States, 2005–2013." *Morbidity and Mortality Weekly Report* 63, no. 47 (2014):1108–12, https://www.cdc.gov/mmwr/preview/mmwrhtml/mm6347a4.htm.

will work with you on the cost. It may be worth every cent for the enhanced quality of care that you will receive.

MENTAL AND EMOTIONAL HEALTH

You need to pay attention to more than your physical health if you are to take care of yourself so that you can be there for others. We know that we need to eat right and exercise if we are to maintain our bodies—and likewise we need to take active steps to maintain our health, both emotionally and mentally. We must be sound of both mind and body if we are to develop meaningful relationships and deal with the many challenges that come into everyone's life.

The Centers for Disease Control and Prevention (CDC) recognizes the connection between physical well-being and emotional and mental well-being.[9] To function well, the body and the mind depend on each other—and that is why taking care of yourself physically is a big part of the solution when you feel emotional or mental distress.

Severe stress, the CDC warns, can be overwhelming to the point where you have trouble taking care of yourself and your family. It can result in eating and sleeping disorders that worsen

---

9   "Well-Being Concepts," Centers for Disease Control and Prevention, last
    modified May 31, 2016, https://www.cdc.gov/hrqol/wellbeing.htm.

the situation—and therefore the agency advises healthy, well-balanced meals, regular exercise, and plenty of sleep to help keep life's problems in perspective.

Common reactions to intense stress are sadness and anxiety, guilt and irritability, depression, and inability to concentrate. Physical symptoms can include headaches, back pain, stomach ailments, and a variety of other reactions. People under emotional distress are at greater risk of substance abuse.

If you or someone you know is experiencing a mental health issue, there are many sources of help. Symptoms can be similar to stress reactions, but they may be even more severe, to the point of doing harm to oneself or others. The daily tasks of life—taking care of yourself and your children, getting to work or to school, can seem too much to contemplate.

The Department of Health and Human Services points out that one in five US adults in a recent year's survey experienced a mental health issue; one in ten young people had a period of major depression; and one in twenty-five people were living with a serious mental condition such as major depression, bipolar disorder, or schizophrenia.[10] Mental illness is far from rare and should be treated

---

10   "Mental Health Myths and Facts," U.S. Department of Health and Human Services, accessed on August 3, 2017, https://www.mentalhealth.gov/basics/myths-facts/index.html.

by a medical professional. Getting help immediately is essential whenever thoughts turn to suicide, which the HHS reports is the tenth leading cause of death in the United States. The statistics show, however, that fewer than half of adults and fewer than a fifth of children and teens get treatment for diagnosable mental illness.

In many cases, fostering healthy relationships is one of the recommended paths to recovery. To deal with stress, it helps to seek out the support of others—family and friends, or a counselor. For mental health issues, many people have found that peer support groups promote recovery as others who have "been there" share their experiences, strengths, and hopes. A trusted family physician can help to evaluate the condition and suggest referrals to the appropriate mental health services.

A HEALTHY OUTLOOK

In *An Interview with God*, a booklet designed and edited by Reata Strickland, the interviewer asks God what he finds surprising about humans. God responds that they are in a rush to grow up but then they long for their youth; that they lose their health trying to make money, and then spend their money trying to regain their health; and that in their anxiety over the future, they forget the present and therefore live for neither. He concludes: "They live as if they will never die, and they die as if they had never lived."[11]

The words were anonymous when the booklet was published in 2002, but they later were attributed to the writer Jim Brown after Publishers Weekly put out an appeal that the unidentified author step forward. Such is the depth of the passage, however, that some

> *We were designed to live life to its fullest.*

have mistakenly attributed it to the Dalai Lama. In any case, it does reflect a heavenly kind of thinking. We were designed to live life to its fullest.

Those who maintain a sense of purpose and meaning in their lives are likely to feel younger and more vibrant for longer than those who try to get through the years aimlessly. That is why I have emphasized the importance of defining your dreams and pursuing them. That is why you need a plan that sets forth clearly what you hope to accomplish. Not only does that make financial sense, but it makes physical sense.

In the movie *The Bucket List*, Jack Nicholson and Morgan Freeman play two men who each hear from their doctors that they

---

11   Jim Brown, *An Interview with God*, designed and edited by Reata Strickland, (New York: Free Press, 2002).

are terminally ill with cancer. As they talk in the hospital room they share, they resolve to attain their lifelong goals together before they "kick the bucket." To list your goals and dreams is a great step toward holding yourself accountable to accomplishing them. But why wait until your days are numbered? Life is short enough as it is. When you make the most of it, filling it with meaning, you have the kind of healthy outlook that keeps the blood pumping.

> *Those who maintain a sense of purpose and meaning in their lives are likely to feel younger and more vibrant for longer than those who try to get through the years aimlessly.*

WHAT YOU NEED TO KNOW

→ You should take reasonable steps to maintain good health—physical, mental, and emotional—so that you have the stamina to reach for your dreams with vigor.

→ Remember the importance of eating right, exercising, getting plenty of sleep, and keeping away from tobacco. You should get regular checkups to monitor your health.

→ Find the right trusted doctor.

→ Those who develop a healthy outlook on life, with a sense of purpose and meaning and clear goals, are likely to keep feeling young and vibrant.

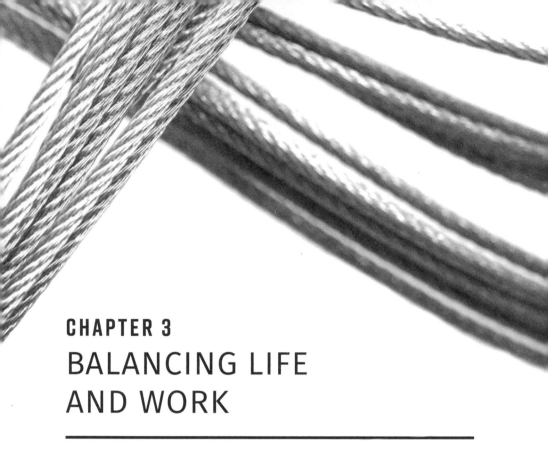

CHAPTER 3
BALANCING LIFE AND WORK

*Most of us spend too much time on what is urgent
and not enough time on what is important.*

—STEPHEN R. COVEY

I had to smile as I reviewed the notes I had been taking on my voice recorder while working on this chapter early on a January morning. I had been doing triple duty: trying to meet a publishing deadline, taking care of my seven-year-old son, Luca, who was home with a cold, and seeing my ten-year-old daughter, Ella, off to school. The recorder picked up snippets of conversation:

Me: "Ella, you need to be getting ready. The bus will be here in fifteen minutes, okay?"

Ella: "What kind of shoes should I wear?"

Me: "Well, wear your sneakers. There's no more snow. Just be sure to get them on ..."

Me: "Luca, did you drink all of your apple juice?"

Luca: "Ok, Dad, going to do it now."

And so forth. It was only the typical back-and-forth between parent and child on a bustling school morning—and that's the point. Later, as I went back to my writing, I realized that those routine words on the recorder were not so much an interruption as they were an illustration of what I was trying to say in this chapter: life is all about being there for what really matters. It's about finding the right balance between work, family, and self.

For mornings like that, my wife Heather and I could hire a babysitter to take our place, but we have decided that we should put a priority on spending time with our kids. One or the other of us, whenever possible, will arrange to be there. And though I didn't get much done on this book that morning, I did something that mattered more than writing a few paragraphs: I got to be a dad.

I have often observed that many people—businesspeople, in particular—have trouble finding the proper balance. As they try to devote time to everything, they spread themselves thin. Something gets neglected. Perhaps it is their business, perhaps it is their family—and sometimes, that something is themselves. They may neglect their health, for example, or give up on dreams. One of my great friends and clients, Stephen, each year makes time for boating with his family. During hunting season, he is sure to build in time for his personal passion of duck hunting. Another one of my best friends from college, David, is a big believer in setting aside time for himself for periods of personal reflection and for personal interests while always continuing to be there for his family and his clients.

You cannot really find contentment unless you identify all that is important to you and make sure that each priority gets an appropriate amount of your time. It's all part of the pursuit of happiness. Yes, you should enjoy the satisfaction of a thriving business, but if that is your only focus, what will you do if the workplace loses its allure and your work begins to feel like drudgery? Yes, you can get much joy from your devotion to your loved ones, but if you ignore your business and it fades, how will you take care of your family? True happiness lies in a well-rounded life.

THE URGENT AND THE IMPORTANT

Dwight D. Eisenhower spoke of two kinds of problems—the urgent and the important. The urgent ones do not tend to be the important ones, and the important ones do not tend to be urgent. The "Eisenhower matrix" for determining priorities in decision making has often been represented as four boxes: in one box are the things that are both important and urgent; in the second, things that are important but not urgent; in the third, things that are not important but are urgent; and in the fourth, things that are neither important nor urgent.

Stephen Covey further developed that matrix in his 1994 book *First Things First*. He wrote that decisions should be guided not just by the clock but also by the compass. In other words, the clock of scheduling is not enough; we need the compass of purpose and values. He referred to the Eisenhower matrix for evaluating tasks by their level of urgency and importance, placing the priority on activities that support long-term goals. When deciding what to do and when, we should ask ourselves whether we are advancing the things that matter most to us. They may not seem urgent, but they ultimately will be of utmost importance.

Decisions become easier when we place them in the context of our values. When we know what comes first in life, we do not get lost in the fog of indecision. We can avoid the stress that arises from a confliction of convictions.

One night recently, my uncle was admitted to the hospital and my mother and I wanted to visit him there. I had a list of twenty phone calls to potential clients who were waiting to hear from me that evening, and of course I must attend to such matters if I expect my business to do well. But I must also attend to family matters if I expect our relationships to do well,

> *Decisions become easier when we place them in the context of our values. When we know what comes first in life, we do not get lost in the fog of indecision. We can avoid the stress that arises from a confliction of convictions.*

and that is a value of greater importance. The Carriero crest emphasizes "family," but it does not say "never reschedule a business call."

My clarity of values helped me to act confidently. My first allegiance was my loyalty to the loved ones in my life. I wasn't blowing off my business responsibilities. I was attending first to the most important business at hand, and that was my family relationships. I was easily able to adjust my schedule to make those calls the next morning.

A MODEL CALENDAR

Time management is a crucial aspect of living efficiently—and that means you need a calendar that is comprehensive so that you encompass the needs of family and self as well as work. It also must be flexible so that you can adjust it depending on the shifting priorities of the moment. Things come up. Conflicts will arise, and they must be weighed by their level of urgency and importance. As the keeper of your calendar, you must adjust to life as it happens. A clear set of values should be the determining factor.

I keep a model calendar on which I designate "focus days," "buffer days," and "free days." I mark the calendar using a different color for each. Focus days are those in which I concentrate on what is most essential for growing my business, such as appointments with clients and speaking engagements. On focus days, I am primarily concerned with productivity. Buffer days are for what I call "cleanup," taking care of various responsibilities such as organizing, conducting team meetings, educating, and the like. On buffer days, I am more in the mode of preparation and development and long-range planning. Free days are those in which I engage in no work activity. Those are days of rejuvenation. They are for personal and family time.

I have found that a schedule like that is the best way to boost productivity. It builds a structure for work/life balance, and from that structure comes a greater sense of freedom. One of my mentors, Tom Nicolosi, shared the idea of the model calendar with me. He told me that it helped him greatly after getting to a point in his career where he felt he was spinning his wheels.

The concept of the free days, focus days, and buffer days originated with the Strategic Coach founder Dan Sullivan. A calendar that accommodates those three distinct elements will encourage the balance that we all need in our pursuit of happiness. I find that those buffer days help me make the most of my focus days and allow me to enjoy the free days without distraction.

As I write this, for example, I am preparing for a busy focus day with a variety of business-generating activities on my schedule. Coming up later in the week are four free days in Vermont—and those days, by and large, will be free of the e-mails and phone calls that would pull me away from that precious family time. At other times, I schedule activities for myself—enjoying a round of golf, for example.

The balance comes from the structure. A single calendar encompasses the needs of self, business, and family. I am able to anticipate and schedule, for example, the time I spend each spring coaching baseball for my son, making sure that the model calendar makes room for that. It helps me keep a perspective on the important things in life. It keeps me from feeling overwhelmed by the daily swirl of things that seem urgent. Everything is in its place, and there is a place for everything. I am not sacrificing my business needs, or my family needs, or my personal needs. I am enhancing each of those areas.

Depending on where you are in life, your model calendar likely will look much different from mine. The calendar of someone managing a growing business while raising a young family will of course have different areas of focus than the calendar of someone who is heading into retirement. We all have different priorities, so there can be no prescriptions for a model calendar. What is right for you is what will lead to happiness.

> *What matters most here is the concept of planning for balance. Without that structure, we could end up depleted by daily demands and lack the energy for what is most important.*

What matters most here is the concept of planning for balance. Without that structure, we could end up depleted by daily demands and lack the energy for what is most important. Many people say that they like to be spontaneous—but unfortunately, that often means they are spontaneously stomping out fires.

In my own family's model calendar, we identify key activities, looking at each week, each month, and the entire year in advance. We gain a sense of reassurance knowing that we have considered the big picture and that we are staying on track. Business and family priorities are clear. The calendar significantly improved my work productivity, but at the same time I know that I am not neglecting my personal needs and growth. As things come up, the calendar flexes. As a family, we think it through. If a school science fair happens to be on the same evening that I have scheduled a client event, we can make the appropriate adjustment to accommodate what is important, and far enough in advance so that no one is inconvenienced.

Day/Time	Sunday	Monday	Tuesday	Wednesday	Thursday	Friday	Saturday
	Free Day	Buffer Day	Focus Day	Focus Day	Focus Day	Focus Day	Buffer Day
4:45 AM		Wake up	Wake up	Wake up	Wake up	Wake up	
5:00 AM		Read 1.5 Hrs	Read 1.5 Hrs	Read 1.5 Hrs	Read 1.5 Hrs	Read 1.5 Hrs	
6:30 AM		Exercise	Exercise	Exercise	Exercise	Exercise	
7:00 AM		Ella & Luca Time	Ella & Luca Time	Ella & Luca Time	Ella & Luca Time	Ella & Luca Time	
7:30 AM							
8:00 AM							
8:30 AM		Head to office	Head to office	Head to office	Head to office	Head to office	
9:00 AM		Rocco Prep Time	OPEN/Research	OPEN/Research	Call's or Apt's	OPEN/Research	
9:30 AM		For Monday Meetings	Case Work	Case Work		Case Work	
10:00 AM			Call's or Apt's	Call's or Apt's	Call's or Apt's	Call's or Apt's	
10:30 AM		Paul & Rocco 1-1					
11:00 AM		Jo Ann & Rocco 1-1	Call's or Apt's	Call's or Apt's	Call's or Apt's	Call's or Apt's	
11:30 AM		Team Mtg 1 X Monthly					
12:00 PM		OPEN/Research	OPEN/Research	OPEN/Research	OPEN/Research	COI Lunch/Office Visit	
12:30 PM		Case Work	Case Work	Case Work	Case Work	Weekly	
1:00 PM		Call's or Apt's	Call's or Apt's	Call's or Apt's	Call's or Apt's		
1:30 PM		Call's or Apt's					
2:00 PM		Merdith & Rocco 1-1	Call's or Apt's	Call's or Apt's	Call's or Apt's		
2:30 PM		Call's or Apt's					
3:00 PM		Bryan & Rocco 1-1	Call's or Apt's	Call's or Apt's	Call's or Apt's	Call's or Apt's	
3:30 PM		OPEN/Research					
4:00 PM		Case Work	OPEN/Research	OPEN/Research	OPEN/Research	OPEN/Research	
4:30 PM		Nicole & Rocco 1-1	Case Work	Case Work	Case Work	Case Work	
5:00 PM			SPRING BASEBALL	Family Night/Date Night	SPRING BASEBALL		
5:30 PM	Review & Plan	Review & Plan	Review & Plan	Review & Plan	Review & Plan	Review & Plan	
6:00 PM			Events	1X per month Date Night	Events		
6:30 PM			1-2 X Monthly		2 X Monthly		
7:00 PM			Workshop		Workshop		
7:30 PM							
9:00 PM							
9:30 PM	Sleep	Sleep	Sleep	Sleep	Sleep		

How often do children grow up to feel that mom or dad never seemed to have time to spend with them, that they were always working or too busy to come to their ball games or look over their homework? And how often do mom or dad look back with regrets that they didn't spend that time? To build a great business and become well known and respected in the community is all fine and well, but what about the rest of it? Is there balance? These are the matters that we must think about, while we still have the time. We need to plan it out.

In her book *The Top Five Regrets of the Dying*, Bronnie Ware wrote about her observations from her years as a hospice nurse. In their final days, she said, people gain great clarity about their lives and what they might have done differently. Their most common regret is that they had failed to pursue their own dreams as they tried to meet the expectations of others. The second most common regret, particularly among men, was that they had worked so much and so hard that they had sacrificed time with their families. They felt they had been on a treadmill, missing the moments that mattered. The other three common regrets express a similar theme of longing for balance: *I wish I'd had the courage to express my feelings. I wish I'd stayed in touch with my friends. I wish I'd let myself be happy.*

We see again that happiness, far from being a selfish pursuit, is a selfless one. Deep in our souls, we desire what matters most. In their final moments, people are not saying they wished they might have fit in a few more work meetings. They are not pondering the performance of their portfolios. They are looking back at how they treated themselves and at what portion of their hearts they shared with loved ones. That is what they wish they had jotted down on the calendar over the many years gone by.

ONE BIG LIFE

On that January morning, having finally seen my daughter and son out the door to school, I turned my attention back to writing this chapter. Reviewing my notes on the recorder, I heard this:

Me: "The bus will be here in only five minutes."

Ella: "Yeah, we know what time it is."

Me: "Ella, do you need your saxophone today? I'll put it here by the door …"

Me: "Luca, are you ready for the spelling test?"

Luca: "Dad, can we practice later together?"

Me: "Yeah, bud, let's make it happen."

Without balance, we cannot be happy, and without happiness what was the point of making all that money? It's a matter of priority, and devotion to family does not mean the business must suffer. Frankly, both do better.

The recorder had captured something more important than the words I was writing for this book—it had captured the script of parenthood. On that recording I didn't just hear myself saying, "It's important to take the time to be a dad." I heard myself being a dad.

It's all one big life. Without balance, we cannot be happy, and without happiness what was the point of making all that money? It's a matter of priority, and devotion to family does not mean the business must suffer. Frankly, both do better. In attending to the needs of your loved ones—and that includes yourself—you capture the joy of living that makes it all worthwhile.

Special time together pays dividends. Your calendar should include date nights with your spouse, for example. After all, it was the marriage that came first, and the family depends on its strength. It is important, as well, to schedule outings with each of your children. And in between those special times, as life happens, we must make the most of it.

WHAT YOU NEED TO KNOW

→ True happiness comes from a well-balanced life in which you give the appropriate attention to self, family, and business.

→ What often seem to be the most urgent matters at hand are often not the most important ones. In every decision, consider what is most meaningful.

→ To find the right balance, it helps to develop a calendar that includes sufficient time for personal, family, and business activities.

SECOND CORD: YOUR BUSINESS

*The biggest mistake a small business can
make is to think like a small business.*

—**POST FILM DESIGN**

When my father became ill and could no longer run his tailor shop, he did not have a succession plan for what would become of the business. In fact, he *was* the business. The clientele were loyal to my father more than to the facility itself. From time to time he had tried to employ other tailors, but those didn't work out. Often, he had to redo their work to keep the customers satisfied. They expected his special touch.

After he passed, we brought in a replacement hoping to keep the operation going, but he didn't have the connections with the community and the customers that my father had maintained, and he didn't want to put in the necessary hours. My father had worked long days and weekends, and it was hard to find anyone willing to see the job as more than a nine-to-five stint.

A year later we closed the shop, and that was the end of the business that had supported the family for all those years. I was my parents' only child, but it had not been my ambition to take over the shop. I had gone on to my own career. Nor was there another employee of the business who had been groomed as a successor.

I would have loved to see the tailor shop survive. Everyone in town, it seemed, had known "Paul the Tailor," which was both their name for my father and the name of the shop. I probably could have found another tailor and tried again to see if it would work out, but it was becoming clear that the effort would be at the expense of my personal life, my family life, and even my existing business.

And so I considered the values that were involved in this situation. Keeping the shop open just wasn't in line with them. I would have lost the life balance that I knew was so crucial to success and happiness. Being with my family on a Saturday took priority over being at the tailor shop. I know that my father would have wanted me to be home with my family, not laboring seven days a week.

To provide a retirement income for my mother, we took a different tack. My father had long since purchased the building that housed the business, but it needed updates and renovations. I decided to restore the hundred-year-old building as a rental. That income now helps to support my mother reliably and comfortably.

For years, my father had practiced his profession and nurtured his business. From him I learned many of the good practices that I bring to my own career as a tailor of financial plans. I also learned something that he did not do, and that was to develop an exit plan.

In the end, he took good care of his family, as he had always done. That's what mattered most, but it could have gone smoother with more foresight. As I consider the future of my own business, and the ones that so many of my clients operate, I want the transition to be seamless. I want for them, and for my own family, something better than my father had. Though he took care of his family and his business, I wish he had also focused more on himself. Seldom did he take days off or vacations, except to return to Italy on occasion to see his siblings and his nieces and nephews there.

Your business is like your child. You nurture it from infancy through its youth and into maturity.

Your business is like your child. You nurture it from infancy through its youth and into maturity. As such, it is an essential part of the three-cord approach. In this section, we will examine how a thriving business, given the right attention and kept in the proper perspective, strengthens the cord of life.

CHAPTER 4
YOUR BUSINESS EXIT PLAN

Every exit is an entry somewhere else.
—TOM STOPPARD

Many business owners, having devoted decades to the growth of their baby, feel confused and uncertain about what the "end" will look like. As they start to think of retirement coming up in a decade or so, they wonder how it will happen. Will the business pass on to one or more of the children? Will a key employee be in a position to take over? Or will an outside buyer in the same industry purchase the business?

I have seen many great businesses that have yet to develop an exit strategy. A lot of them certainly could attract the interest of young people who would love to have the opportunity to become the new owner. These are businesses with existing customers and brands—but they have not taken the time to consider how the business will transition from their hands into someone else's.

If you are old enough that retirement is increasingly on your mind, then it is high time to pay attention to what will become of your business. If you have presumed that it will go to the children, for example, you must ask yourself whether they are truly prepared. Have you taken the time to teach them the particulars of your business, or even the basics of how to run one? Have you introduced them to your clients and customers so that they can begin to develop that essential bond of trust? Have you given any thought to the financial details of the transaction so that it benefits all parties, including the ability of the business itself to endure?

And are any of the children even interested in taking over the business? What are their passions? Just because you might imagine that they would like to spend the next several decades doing what you do doesn't mean they relish the prospect—whether it's running a material supply company, construction company, service company, restaurant, or professional services practice, or even becoming a doctor or a tailor. Or do you somehow intend to force them to give up their own dreams?

I have sometimes observed that happening. The founders of the business want to keep their own passion alive, but it is not one that their children share. If the children feel they have no choice in the matter, they often begin to resent it over time. *I could have been a doctor*, they tell themselves, or *I was born to be an engineer, not a shopkeeper—but now I'm stuck here.*

If you do have one or more children who want to stay in the business in one way or another, what is the best way for them to get a good start? Should they first get a college degree, or work in a related business for a while to see how they like it? Many business owners believe, for good reason, that young people should spend some time to find out what life is like out there before deciding whether to follow in their footsteps. It's a major commitment, and it is a good idea to get a feel first for the inner workings. Young people need the reassurance of knowing they were free to follow their own passions and that they chose the business on their own volition, without pressure. They should not feel that failing to join the fold would somehow let the family down. It should be their chosen path.

Sometimes it is a key employee, not one or more of the children, who will become the successor. That is another common route for business transition. Perhaps a longtime employee would like the opportunity to purchase the controlling interest and take over. If so, what are the logistics for making that happen?

Another common exit strategy is to sell to an outside buyer in the same industry, making sure in the years leading to the sale that the business is primed to get the best price possible. Many times that is the best option, to make a clean break from the business. The seller might continue to work in the business for a year or two after the sale to help with the transition, and then make a clean break. I have seen many cases where that works best.

DOING IT RIGHT

There is so much at stake in doing this right. Failure to attend to these matters can result in a loss of significant wealth—and even destroy a business. You will have two major responsibilities: building transferable value throughout the course of running your business and identifying and addressing the risks along the way that could be harmful to the welfare of your business.

A common mistake is to sell for the wrong reasons. Perhaps someone comes along with an offer, and the owner jumps for it—but the timing is premature. Sometimes I see people selling a business after their children have changed their minds about joining it. The sale seems to be motivated by disappointment or desperation. Owners need to consider whether they are selling for the right reason—which is that they feel it is time to focus their energies on something else in life that they find exciting.

It is essential, when anticipating the sale, to spruce up the business—and that means both the windows and the books. You want to do everything you can to increase the curb appeal, because that can help you to get a premium price. It's time to take care of all that long-delayed maintenance. It's time to scrub the floors. First impressions count.

This is also the time to start cleaning up your financials. Your final years of ownership should be the most profitable ones in your career. That's what you want prospective buyers to see on your books. They will want the reassurance that they, too, can produce such an outcome. If necessary, do some housecleaning with your personnel, as well. You should have the right people in the right jobs, and your payroll expense should be in line with the typical percentage for your type of business.

WHAT IS THE BUSINESS WORTH?

Many owners are unrealistic about their business's value—they presume it is worth more than it is. They have emotional ties to their life's work, and they imagine that others will feel the same way. They want prospective buyers to appreciate all that they have done, which they very well might—but when negotiating on price, you can be sure that buyers will be looking for reasons that the business might be worth less, not more.

Many business owners don't have an official valuation, and without one they essentially are guessing at what they might get. They have built the company from scratch and have operated it competently, but to a buyer, a business is worth only what the owner can show in assets and income. A valuation expert who knows the industry well can produce an accurate estimate based on several years of statements and an assessment of cash flow, assets, and profitability. That is the figure that will help the owner determine whether the time has come to sell and retire.

ANTICIPATING THE TAXES

It's a big question: How much of your negotiated price will you have left after taxes? Whether you are dealing with the capital gains tax, ordinary income tax, or depreciation recapture, the sale can be structured in many ways to potentially reduce the tax bite. Generally, however, the business owner's area of expertise lies somewhere other than the complexities of the tax code. That is why it is important to bring in tax and financial professionals when selling or transitioning a business.

Some business owners are able to save on taxes by gifting stock in the company to their children if they are interested in running it. To produce a retirement income, they might set up a deferred compensation agreement or similar arrangement. The gifting option, of course, usually is desirable only when the transition is within the family—but with an outside buyer, as well, taxes are certain to be part of the negotiations.

GETTING AN EARLY START

All of this needs to be considered well before it happens. You should weigh all of the options and set a formal plan in place. Your succession planning needs to be accomplished while you are alive and alert and fully cognizant of all the details. Though that might seem obvious, it is often not how it turns out—and the succession planning cannot be done posthumously.

The succession planning should begin, in fact, not long after the business itself is launched. Once it is clear that the business will be a moneymaker with something valuable to offer, it is time to protect that interest. In the case of partnerships, the exit strategy should be considered even before launching the business.

> *Your succession planning needs to be accomplished while you are alive and alert and fully cognizant of all the details.*

Such decisions get down to the purpose that the business will be serving. Why are you building it? Is it existing just to provide a current income? Is the intention to grow it, and if so, why? Is the ultimate goal to provide a solid retirement income, or are you also building a family enterprise and legacy? Matters of such importance deserve your deep consideration. You should not just wait until you're getting tired and want to move on before figuring out what to do—because by then, you do not really have enough time to do it right.

WHAT YOU NEED TO KNOW

→ What will become of your business after you hand over the reins? Whether it will stay in the family or you will sell it to an outside buyer or key employee, you need to get an early start on developing a sensible exit strategy.

→ As you anticipate selling your business, you should spruce it up—and that means everything from cleaning the windows to cleaning up the books. First impressions count if you are to get a premium price.

→ You should get a professional valuation of what your business is worth, and weigh the tax considerations involved in a sale. You need to fully understand that information before you can decide whether the time has come to retire and pursue the next exciting chapter of your life.

CHAPTER 5
BUILDING A RETIREMENT PORTFOLIO

It's not how much money you make, but how much money you keep, how hard it works for you, and how many generations you keep it for.

—ROBERT KIYOSAKI

Imagine that, as a business owner, you have sold your company and the day has come when you are receiving a check for a lump sum that represents your life's work. How will you feel? This is certainly a new direction. For many years, you have depended on the proceeds of your business for a reliable income that allowed you to raise your family while building for a future. Now what?

If you are like many business owners in this position, the future still feels undefined even though the sale is over. Getting that check was supposed to represent the high water mark of your business career, but you still have many questions. And the primary one is likely to be this: Will there be enough money, after the toll of taxes, to produce a lifelong income that will maintain the lifestyle to which you and your family have been accustomed?

Wealth preservation is top of mind for most business owners who are looking to sell. That is their primary objective. They are seeking to position their liquid assets in a way that will allow them to create the kind of income that they were receiving while operating the business. They want to replace that income, and so they are trying to decide which investment tools they should use.

As they negotiate the price, the owners are thinking: If I were to just keep running the business, how long would it take me to make the amount of money I would get in this offer? They are trying to decide whether it's worthwhile. Many business owners want a multiplier of four to six times annual net earnings. If they are offered only two or three, they figure that they can just continue to run the business for another few years, get that amount in income—and still own the business.

They want to receive enough money from the sale, in other words, that they can do something significant with it while maintaining the kind of lifestyle they expect. Otherwise they figure that they might as well just continue making the money from the business. Let's say you are earning $1 million a year from your business, and someone offers you $2–3 million. You don't get too excited because you can make that much just by keeping the doors open another couple years. But if someone offers you $7 million, or $10 million, you start to think of all the things you could do with that money: You could invest it, or start another business, or do something special for your family. No longer are you thinking: *Why bother?* Now you are thinking: *what an opportunity!*

MAKING THE MOST OF THE SALE

A business owner certainly has much on his or her mind when negotiating that sales price. There tends to be three competing considerations:

- *Is the deal in the best interest of my own financial future and my family?*

- *Is the deal in the best interest of the company's ability to thrive in the future?*

- *Is the deal structured so that my successors will be able to make enough money to succeed?*

The way the sales deal is designed will depend a lot on who the buyer is. If the sale is to the children or to key employees, it is likely that those buyers will not be able to come up with a large down payment. They may be able to get a loan to purchase part of the company stock, but it may be necessary to sell the company to them over a period of years as they make monthly payments. They will need to have enough training and knowledge to run the company wisely and continue to make those payments for many years. That is an important consideration: the business must be able to produce sufficient annual cash flow for the buyers to continue making those payments.

If the sale is to someone else in the industry, the business probably can be sold for a somewhat higher price, which can be made in one or two payments. A big consideration there is whether enough money will remain after taxes to provide the seller with an adequate retirement income. You should consult with a tax advisor to make sure you have considered all the ramifications.

How to divvy up the taxes between buyer and seller is often an important part of the negotiations. For example, you might be able to facilitate the sale by allowing the buyer to pay some of the price in the form of compensation income, guaranteed for a certain period. All parties will have a keen interest in keeping taxes down, and the goal should be to do so in a way that is fair to all—the buyer, the seller, and the business itself.

As you can see, there is much to talk about at the negotiating table besides just the sale price. Sometimes, as the seller considers an offer, the negotiations can include creative ways to compensate the owner other than just through the direct proceeds of the sale. This has been accomplished through a variety of methods—the former owner, for example, might get a deferred compensation agreement, a consulting contract, or a position on the board of directors.

Although most sellers do prefer the lump sum, all of those alternatives can become income sources for retirement. There are many ways for the seller to get "paid" that can also help the successors run the business successfully. This can be a particularly important consideration when the business is transferring within the family to the children.

The tax and other considerations can become quite complicated, so it is important to work with professionals who understand all the implications. I have assisted clients in those negotiations. We consult with a tax advisor to lay out the options and then assess how they would affect the client's financial plan. Are they able to meet their goals and their objectives under each of those scenarios?

A RELIABLE LIFETIME INCOME

However the deal is structured, a successful businessperson who has completed a sale will have a significant sum in hand at some point—and the question now becomes how to invest those proceeds to produce a reliable lifetime income. The goal is to create income streams that will last through the many years of retirement—but with enough growth to keep ahead of inflation, which inevitably will take a steady toll during those decades.

In an ideal world, many business owners say they would like a situation in which they continued to own a business but would not have any employees to manage. They might accomplish that through private equity investments in small businesses where they become an equity partner. That's one possibility among many on how to invest the proceeds of your sale.

Let's take a general look at some other means—real estate, a qualified retirement account, and assets outside the business—by which you could build that reliable retirement portfolio after the sale of your business. In many cases, as you will see, it is important to start building it long before the sale.

Real estate

Many businesspeople own the real estate where their company is located and already have the mortgage paid off. If the deal is properly structured, the business portion can be sold and the new owner can continue to rent the real estate.

That rental income is normally a very good income source for both the former business owner and their spouse in the retirement years. It can also be an asset that can be divided among children and grandchildren or other beneficiaries.

A qualified retirement account

When they reach that point in their career when they are thinking about selling their company, many businesspeople have invested a significant amount of assets in some type of qualified retirement plan. Generally, it is considered to be good practice to contribute 10 to 15 percent of one's income to a tax-deductible retirement account for at least twenty or thirty years, or until final retirement. Most people, however, did not start contributing to such an account early enough, and they do not put in sufficient assets.

The traditional IRA and the Roth IRA are two of the primary qualified accounts for retirement savings that offer significant tax benefits, but they differ greatly in how they operate. In short, with the traditional IRA you save on taxes during your working years when you put your money in; and with the Roth, you save on taxes during retirement when you take the money out. The amount that you put into a traditional IRA is generally tax-deductible up front, during the year in which you make the contribution, but during retirement your withdrawals will be taxed at the ordinary income tax rates at that time. The Roth IRA differs in that you get no immediate tax break for your contributions, but the earnings and withdrawals generally will be tax-free if you meet all the IRS requirements.

Which makes sense for you? It will depend on whether you expect to pay a higher or a lower income tax rate during retirement than you do today. Which will be greater—today's tax rate on your Roth contributions, or the rate you will pay during retirement when you withdraw from a traditional IRA? If you expect that it will be the latter, you may appreciate the tax-free nature of a Roth that comes when all requirements have been met.

It's hard to predict where tax rates will be decades into the future, but consider that today's federal rates are at a historic low and we are facing a huge national deficit. And you should ask yourself whether you truly expect to be making less money in retirement. Many retirees find that their income increases and they move into a higher bracket, defeating the purpose of tax deferral.

Another big difference between a traditional IRA and a Roth involves the rules for withdrawal. With the traditional IRAs, you must begin taking your required minimum distributions (RMDs) at age seventy and a half, or else you will face a 50 percent penalty of the amount not withdrawn. With the Roth, no withdrawals are required. The money in the account can continue to grow throughout your retirement, allowing you to leave a sizable sum to your heirs, free of income taxes, though once your heirs have inherited from you they are subject to RMDs.

After selling their business, many people will roll all their retirement accounts into one IRA and manage it based on their goals. However, keep in mind that managing retirement assets requires a far different approach than the way a business typically is managed. These investments need to be protected from the major fluctuations of the stock market and the economy.

Assets outside the business

Many business owners approach retirement with 70 or 80 percent of their net worth wrapped up in the company. Over the years, they tended to plow their profits back into the company so that they could buy more inventory or make improvements and expansions. That can be good for the company, but it also means that the company must be sold for a premium if the family is to retire comfortably. All those years of putting the money back into the business often means that insufficient personal assets have been saved elsewhere that could provide an income to last for what easily could be three decades of retirement.

How can you avoid that problem? It would be a good idea, when you are in your forties or fifties, to open a personal investment account. At that point, you could begin taking some of your profits out of the company and buying high-quality, long-term stock and bond assets. You may also be interested in purchasing farmland, apartment buildings, office buildings, and other types of income-producing real estate. A financial plan designed with multiple sources of income is much stronger than simply depending on the continued success of a single business.

I have often shown clients a diagram to help them see the many sources from which they might replace the income from their business. If the business had been generating $1 million a year, for example, the diagram might show $500,000 from market investments, $250,000 from real estate income, and $250,000 from investing in other small businesses, or however else the capital from the sale could be put to good use.

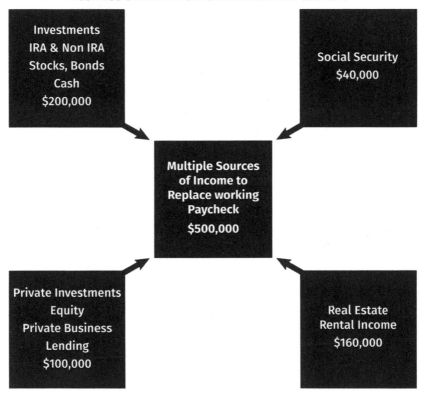

Starting early is good advice all around. The more years you have in front of you, the more time you will have not only to grow your business, but also to grow assets outside your business to add to the proceeds once you sell it or transfer it. Long before you sell, you should be diversifying so that your assets are protected from the whims of the economy.

WHAT YOU NEED TO KNOW

→ For most business owners looking to sell, the primary consideration is this: Will the proceeds after taxes be sufficient to produce a lifelong income to support their lifestyle?

→ While building your business, you should make sure that you also invest elsewhere so that all your assets are not concentrated in the company. That way, your retirement lifestyle will not be entirely dependent on how much you get from the sale.

→ Investments in real estate, qualified retirement accounts, and small businesses are among the strategies often used after the sale of a business. You should generally strive to preserve your wealth from the fluctuations of the market and the economy.

CHAPTER 6
RISKS TO YOUR WEALTH

Risk comes from not knowing what you're doing.

—WARREN BUFFET

The former owner of a telecommunications company told me how it felt to ride the dot-com roller coaster at the turn of the new millennium. He had ascended to the peak and managed to sell his company in time to receive a large sum. He cashed in before the bubble burst—but it was what he did with that cash that did him in. He began working with a financial advisor who led him into a variety of risky investments, and then came the plunge. At least half of his dollars vanished.

During that feverish time, such scenarios were not uncommon—and they highlight the importance of understanding just how risky the market can become. There's a fundamental, but essential, lesson to be learned here. When you are managing the money that you expect to see you through all your days, be prudent with it. You face many risks, and the market is only one of them.

> *There's a fundamental, but essential, lesson to be learned here. When you are managing the money that you expect to see you through all your days, be prudent with it. You face many risks, and the market is only one of them.*

That doesn't mean you should take the mattress stuffing approach: your assets do need to grow, or inflation will pick your pocket. The market represents our collective productivity as a nation, and if you believe that it is generally on the way up, you will feel confident in taking calculated risks that are likely to produce a healthy rate of growth for your portfolio over time. You are wisely putting your dollars to work for you. But if you are out to make as much money in your investments as you possibly can, and as soon as you can, you will be facing risks that could turn good fortune into bad.

If you do take a hit as a result of your questionable choices and get caught in the inevitable cycles of the economy, then you need to face the risk that your emotions could worsen your situation. After the recent economic contractions, some investors pulled out of the market entirely—and missed out on an impressive recovery. Fear and greed can be the biggest risks of all to your wealth.

One of my retired clients was a chief financial officer for various publicly traded construction, manufacturing, and industrial companies during his career. He certainly knows his way around in the financial world. "I can do all this stuff on my own," he told me, "but the reason why I don't is that my emotions always get in the way." He was conceding that we humans are at risk of letting feelings get in the way of logic. Sometimes investors are inclined to think that infinity is the limit, and sometimes they see only darkness down the road. They may respond with what they believe is common sense, but that from-the-gut approach often gets them into trouble. They buy high, and they sell low, which is hardly the prescription for success.

In this chapter we will look at the array of risks to your wealth. Most people think of financial risk as what might happen to their money in the markets, and that is true—but that is not all that will determine how you fare. You also need to carefully consider the role of inflation, interest rate fluctuations, taxes, and investment expenses. In Chapter 2, we looked at the importance of taking care of your health. But as we grow old, we in time grow frail. Are you prepared for the prospect that you or your spouse might need long-term care? That can be financially devastating unless you are prepared for it. We will examine growing older, and various ways of dealing with it, in Chapter 8.

An advisor who does more in-depth and comprehensive planning, with whom you have developed a trusting relationship, can help you keep track of all those risks and manage them as part of a complete financial plan for your life. Your advisor can help you determine whether your decisions are working together in your best interest for the long run.

You need the right strategy for handling your portfolio, and it should be based on your goals. If your goal is to reach retirement with financial freedom, you will want the right balance to give you the best chance of getting there. You should not be taking the risk, for example, of pumping all your money into technology, bank, or pharmaceutical stocks. A good advisor will hold you accountable to what you have set out to accomplish.

Life and financial challenges come to every family, and it is our increased longevity that has much to do with many of the risks that we face in retirement. Back in the 1930s, when Social Security was inaugurated and our life expectancy was much shorter, these risks to the retirement portfolio did not seem as severe. After all, many people lived only a few years after their working days were done. Today, when the span of retirement could potentially be as long as the span of those working years, we need to be ever more protective of the money that must see us through.

Your future is at stake. You need to manage your risks, looking for the potential pitfalls along with the opportunities that catch your attention. Through effective planning, you can deal with each of those threats, if you know what they are. You need to identify them. Awareness is the first step. Let's examine some of the forces that could compromise your financial well-being, starting with a closer look at the markets.

INVESTMENT RISK

You can't argue with the math, although sometimes it seems surprising. Consider this: if your portfolio falls by 10 percent, it will need to rise by about 11 percent to get back to even. If you take a 50 percent blow to your investments, you would need to somehow get a 100 percent return the following year to bring your numbers back to where they were.

If you are depending on your portfolio for retirement income and your totals take a tumble for a number of years, you could be forced to sell equities in order to maintain the standard of living that you expected. That further depletes your portfolio value, potentially sending it into a death spiral. You find yourself with less and less money, and you need better and better performance to pull you out of that pit. If you go after riskier investments to feed that need, you could experience a loss and hit rock bottom more quickly.

You should never be forced to sell. You should be divesting at the most advantageous time for you, not because you need the money. When you sell equities at the wrong time, you are also selling their potential—what could have been. Markets do rise, and they do fall—but no one can say with certainty just when that will be. If the bear settles in for a visit during the early years of your retirement, you could be in big trouble if you have no choice but to withdraw your income from a portfolio exposed to the market.

That is the concept of "sequence of returns." Many investors pay rapt attention to the average annual return that is posted for a security. They want to see how it has performed over the last three years or five years. What matters more in retirement, however, is how it has performed in your portfolio, for your purposes. In which order were the good years and the bad years? You are fortunate if the good years come first. If the bad ones came on the cusp of retirement, you might never recover from that early blow.

Let's say you start with a million-dollar balance and high hopes for a prosperous retirement. You immediately face a bad year, ending with $850,000. Another comes along, and another, before the bull comes back into the ring. At that point you may have only half a million left—but your income needs have not diminished, and as you continue to withdraw your money, your fortunes further fall. However, if you turn that sequence of returns around, with the good years coming first and the bad ones later, you could be doing quite well. As you can see, the average annual return is just an average. It reflects historic performance. It doesn't reflect how well the investment will function in your portfolio.

Your dreams and even your lifestyle can be jeopardized unless you anticipate how you are going to draw your retirement income. Always remember that when you take a risk, you potentially could achieve a greater gain—but you also raise your chances of suffering a greater loss. As your risk increases, your likelihood of success declines. Even if you do better than an index, will that necessarily be cause for celebration? If your investments are down

20 percent, will you be telling yourself that at least your loss was less than the S&P 500's loss?

You and your advisor will need to pay attention to whether your portfolio needs to be rebalanced to reflect your original investment goals. Your asset allocation can get out of whack even if you have not bought or sold anything. If it is your strategy, for example, to maintain a moderate portfolio, you will want to make sure that any change in that strategy is purposeful, not happenstance.

Let's say you wanted a portfolio mix that is 60 percent in equities. In time, if those equities do well, they will claim an increasingly large share of your total. That means it's time to readjust. Clients often ask: "Why would we want to sell from areas that are doing well and put that money into the underperforming areas?" Common sense tells them otherwise, and those emotions get in the way again. The answer is that you should be true to your strategy. There is a good chance that those winners are reaching their peak and could soon start to cycle down. The underperformers very well could be getting ready to blossom anew.

Remember: the way to make money in the market is to sell high and to buy low. If an investment is becoming overpriced and more risky, you want less of it. If you see a good deal, you want more of it. Presumably you included all those investments in your portfolio because you believed they would serve you well. Therefore, it makes sense to regularly monitor your portfolio to make sure you are not taking on more risk than you originally planned and that you are seizing opportunities to use some of your profits to buy bargains.

You may have heard of the "rule of 100," often cited as a handy formula for rebalancing your asset allocation. It originated with John Bogle, founder of the Vanguard Group, back when bond funds were considered low risk by nature. Simply subtract your age from 100, the rule says, and the result is the percentage of your portfolio to put in risk investments, with the remainder going to more conservative investments. That means that as you get older and closer to retirement, you will be taking on less risk as you adjust your allocations.

It's not quite that simple, though. What makes sense for you will depend on your personal situation as well as the prevailing economic conditions. And with today's interest rates likely to rise from historic lows, the prospect for bonds is not what it was. Bonds are not necessarily a safe investment, although many people still treat them that way. Bonds, too, entail risk. The best rule of thumb is this: your investment mix should advance your own goals and objectives as you have identified them in your overall financial plan. That is the only appropriate perspective to determine the level of risk that is right for you.

> The best rule of thumb is this: your investment mix should advance your own goals and objectives as you have identified them in your overall financial plan.

A generic rule produces generic results. No single strategy works for everybody. Good advice for one person could be bad for another. What is most important is to consider first what you are aiming to accomplish and to arrange your investments toward that end.

THE TOLL OF INFLATION

Over the decades, inflation has sometimes reached the double digits and sometimes receded to next to nothing—but it has always lurked as a threat to savings and investments, averaging about 3 percent a year over the last century.[12] Like rust, it does its damage slowly and silently and often goes unnoticed until it has eaten a hole in the family budget.

Even at 3 percent, you could soon feel its effects. The car that costs $30,000 today would cost over $40,000 in a decade and

---

12   Tim McMahon, "Long-Term U.S. Inflation," InflationData, April 1, 2014, https://inflationdata.com/Inflation/Inflation_Rate/Long_Term_Inflation.asp.

over $54,000 in twenty years. Consider what you once paid for a movie ticket, or a week's worth of groceries. During the course of a typical retirement, those expenses could easily double again even at a modest inflation rate. Or think of it this way: if you are retiring with $1 million today, a person retiring in twenty-five years will need well over $2 million to maintain the same purchasing power if inflation continues at that typical 3 percent pace.

During the days when you were accumulating wealth, inflation may not have been much on your mind. If you were building a successful business, your income rose as the business grew. Despite inflation, you were able to maintain your purchasing power. Now, in retirement, your investments must keep ahead of inflation. If they do not, you may find your goals increasingly difficult to accomplish. And the inflation of some expenses, such as health care, hit older people particularly hard.

To tame the effects of inflation, you need sufficient growth in your retirement portfolio. If you are so conservative in your investments that they fall short of the inflation rate, you will be losing ground. If inflation is at 3 percent and you are earning only 1.5 percent on your money, you may be playing it too safe. Your buying power is slipping away. To stop the drain, you will need to take a calculated risk with some portion of your money that you

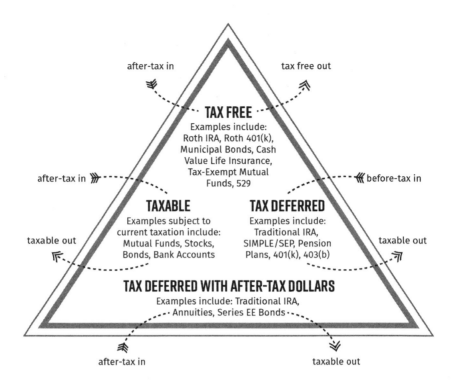

When all three categories are available for your retirement income, you can withdraw just the right blend to keep your tax bracket as low as possible. That means more money in your pocket, since you will have a portion of income that you will not need to declare on your tax return. You can also strategically donate to charity. Because qualified charities are tax exempt, it makes sense to donate from a taxable account and leave the tax-free money to your children and other heirs.

Taxable investments are simply those that will generate an income-tax obligation for the year in which they produce earnings.

A taxable account could include an array of assets such as stocks and their dividends, US treasury bonds, corporate bonds, certificates of deposit, and taxable mutual funds. Each of those, unless included in a qualified tax-deferred plan such as a 401(k) or IRA, will produce income that you must include on your income tax return for the current year. In the case of mutual funds, it is possible for the investor to be subject to tax on income earned in the fund even if the fund lost money during the year. It's known as "phantom income tax": If at any time during the year the fund manager sells a position for a gain, that gain must be distributed among all shareholders on a per share basis. You will be taxed on it, even if you bought into the fund after that transaction, and even if the fund's overall value fell for the year.

Tax-free investments and accounts include municipal bonds, Roth IRAs, 529 education accounts, and some insurance policies. This is money that can grow without subjecting you to taxes. In Chapter 5, we looked at how a Roth can be highly advantageous when developing a flexible portfolio to produce income after the sale of the business. You contribute after-tax dollars to a Roth, and if you follow all the rules and Congress doesn't change them, your income will never be taxed on your investment. Similarly, you can fund a 529 education account with after-tax dollars, and whatever you withdraw will be free of tax—but you must use the money for qualified higher education expenses of the beneficiary. You might also produce a flow of tax-free income from the cash value of a properly structured life insurance policy to which you contributed after-tax money over the years.

Tax-deferred investments are those on which you can postpone taxation by including them in a traditional IRA, a 401(k)-type plan, or tax-deferred annuity. The amount you contribute to a retirement plan can generally be deducted (subject to certain limitations) on your current year's tax return, giving you more disposable income that you presumably could use to invest for even more gains. The government, instead of claiming its share now, is willing to wait until you withdraw the money during retirement. You will then be taxed on both the untaxed amount that you contributed over the years and on the amount that your money has grown. That tax will be based on the prevailing rate at the time as well as your tax bracket. You cannot predict whether that tax rate will be higher or lower so far into the future. As for your tax bracket, the presumption is that you will be in a lower one than during your working years, but that might not be the case at all. Tax-deferred annuities also offer tax deferral, although generally you contribute money on which you already have been taxed and pay nothing further as it grows over time. You will be taxed at ordinary income tax rates on that growth when you withdraw the money—and the IRS requires that you withdraw the growth portion of your account first.

The majority of retirees today have most of their savings tied up in the tax-deferred investments that they set aside in their IRA or 401(k)-type plans. In other words, they lack the tax diversity to most effectively keep down their obligation to the government. This has become increasingly the case as those retirement plans have proliferated over the past four decades. Most retirees do not have a ready source of tax-free assets with which to bolster their retirement income. They are dealing with dollars that have never been taxed, and now, in retirement, they need to withdraw considerably more from their account than the amount they actually need. If a new roof will cost $10,000, for example, the retirement account must cover the tax obligation on top of that—perhaps a total of $12,500. Remember that a portion of those tax-deferred accounts will ultimately go to the government. If you need a spendable income of $75,000 a year, for example, you may need to withdraw $100,000.

Some people try to manage their taxes by converting a traditional IRA into a Roth so that they can enjoy a tax-free income in retirement—but remember that to do so you must immediately pay all the deferred taxes up front on the amount that you are converting. Generally, it makes sense to convert only when you are young enough and have enough years in front of you to feel confident that you will be able to recover from that tax cost. If you convert $1 million, after all, you are left with perhaps $600,000 to $700,000. You will need time to build that back up. Back in 1999, when people were doing the first Roth conversions, many of them were soon slammed by the stock market correction of 2000–2002. Many of those conversions in hindsight were not wise tax decisions; many were reversed as was permitted under the law.

INTEREST RATE RISK

If you are basing your investment decisions on the current interest rate, listen well: that interest rate is certain to change over time, and may not be in your favor.

To tame inflation, the Federal Reserve sometimes tries to cool the economy by raising interest rates. If it sees the need to fend off a recession and stimulate spending, it may lower interest rates. Those rate changes could come steadily throughout the course of a year, or the Fed may leave the rates untouched for months on end.

Even the economists disagree with one another on the direction that interest rates are likely to take, and how far, in any given year.

Investors should not pin their dreams on the interest rates of the moment. Certificates of deposit, for example, once commanded double-digit rates (although even then they were hard-pressed to keep up with double-digit inflation). Not long ago, the average CD rate was still several percent; a million-dollar investment would yield $50,000 or $60,000 a year. With recent rates about 1 percent, how far would that $10,000 a year go toward strengthening your lifestyle?[13]

Interest-rate risk is of particular concern to bond investors, who have a different perspective on the direction of rates. It is a rise in interest rates that depletes a bond's value. It's like a seesaw: As rates rise, bond values fall, and vice versa. Whenever interest rates generally begin to rise, investors look for better deals than those old fixed-rate bonds. When demand is down, prices fall.

When you consider that interest rates have been at historical lows, they are likely to rise toward the historic average. The resulting devaluation of bonds would be greatest for those locked into longer terms. As on the seesaw, what goes up on one side must come down on the other. To reduce the risk of lost value, fixed-

13   Denise Mazzucco, "Historical CD Interest Rates – 1984-2016," Bankrate, last modified April 19, 2016, https://www.bankrate.com/banking/cds/historical-cd-interest-rates-1984-2016/.

income investors should consider a laddering approach, looking at a variety of maturity periods over time.

INVESTMENT EXPENSES IN MUTUAL FUNDS

Many investors pay a lot of attention to the expense ratios of mutual funds and managed accounts. They understandably want to pay as little in fees as possible because that is money that benefits the fund managers and not themselves. They want to make sure they are paying a reasonable amount.

Although that is an important consideration, and you should study the fund or investment prospectus to learn all you can about the stated fees, I believe that a greater concern is investment selection. You need to understand the nature of the product in which you are investing. It is true, for example, that index funds tend to have much lower management expenses because they simply track the performance of various benchmarks. However, that does not mean that you should categorically reject a managed fund with a higher expense ratio. If that fund has a sufficient return to get you where you need to go, then it could very well be the one for you.

In other words, you should be aware of the fees but not base your choice of a fund on them alone. If you select the wrong investment for your purposes, you could be putting your retirement lifestyle at risk. If a fund performs well within your portfolio, and serves your purposes, it can be a good choice over an index fund with a considerably lower return. (Just remember, however, that an investment's track record is no guarantee that it will continue to perform that way. You need to determine the level of market risk that is appropriate for you and your portfolio.)

Fund expenses need to be considered as part of the total return. You need to look at the fees, yes, but also the overall performance within your portfolio. Comprehensive planning will look at the overall picture.

Similarly, while you certainly must pay close attention to your tax obligation, I have seen people become so focused on the taxes and so determined to avoid them that they make unwise decisions in light of their overall financial picture. For example, some real estate owners sold property just before the additional 3.8 percent capital gains tax was instituted for the Affordable Care Act. Had they only waited a few years, they might have made significantly more in a rising real estate market than they ever would have had to pay in taxes. Sometimes such shortsightedness has been called "letting the tax tail wag the investment dog." That dog gets so dizzy it can't see straight.

THE RISK OF HUMAN NATURE

It has been said that the markets rise and fall on greed and fear. Most investors understand, intellectually, that the way to make money is to buy low and sell high. Emotionally, most investors have a hard time sticking to that principle. They ride the wave of euphoria during a bull market, motivated by a desire for greater and greater gain. When the market inevitably slips, they hold on tight, almost in disbelief, and then become fearful and sell—sometimes at the bottom of the cycle, when they have the most to lose.

Wise shoppers everywhere are those who seek out bargains. Unfortunately, many investors will first weed out their weaker performers so that they can buy more of those that have been rallying. That's not bargain hunting. That amounts to shopping for the highest price.

Investor behavior has become a field of social study examining the biases that inform people's decisions. Some of those behaviors are rooted in lifelong impressions, planted in childhood, while others simply reflect human nature. People tend to follow the crowd and run with the herd, for example. They look for information and perspectives that reflect what they already believe. They presume that what has been happening in the market most recently is what is most likely to continue happening. Each of those instincts can result in faulty decisions.

I work with many successful people, some of whom have been financial executives at major corporations. They are truly capable of selecting investments. They choose to work with my practice, however, because they wisely recognize that their own emotions can get in the way of proper long-term planning. Emotional reactions to the market can be an investor's downfall. In the 2008–2009 debacle, for example, some people imagined that the markets might plunge to zero. The doom-and-gloom reports led them to make decisions that seriously compromised their wealth. Ultimately, they floundered because of their fears. They bailed out at the bottom and missed a dramatic recovery. These were smart folks, intellectually. Emotionally, less so.

Perhaps you are a starry-eyed optimist who always expects the best—and who takes on too much risk, leaving your life savings exposed to potential loss. Or perhaps you are so weighed down by pessimism that you hide from risk whenever possible and lose out on one opportunity after another. Maybe you are one of the few who can set emotions and worldview aside and take an impartial approach, based on what makes sense rationally. If you are wise, you will recognize that you are vulnerable to human tendencies that can result in big mistakes. Through awareness, we overcome.

WHAT YOU NEED TO KNOW

→ Our increased longevity has accentuated the financial risks in retirement. Through effective planning, you can deal with each of those threats if you know what they are.

→ Most people think of financial risk as their exposure to the markets, but you also need to carefully consider the role of inflation, interest rate fluctuations, taxes, and investment expenses.

→ Your financial advisor can help you keep track of all those risks and manage them as part of a comprehensive plan for your life.

THIRD CORD: YOUR FAMILY

(**family**) noun

Pronounced / fam-uh-lee

1. The people you surround yourself with and love
    unconditionally

2. One of life's greatest blessings

---

*Making family a top priority will
invariability bring success.*

—ZIG ZIGLAR

Though I was facing a pressing deadline to complete this manu-
script, something else mattered more to me: I needed to make sure
that my mother and my aunt and I made it to church.

I had joined the two of them—my mom is seventy-eight, my aunt, eighty-six—on a trip to Florida, and I wanted to drive them around to the sights and the stores and spoil them a bit. Never mind how busy I was with my career and my writing—this opportunity to make family memories came first. "Family" is prominent on the Carriero crest for good reason.

"Oh, you have so many other things to do, Rocco," they each told me. They didn't want to be a trouble to me. No way could they have been a trouble. They had mentioned that they would like to go to church, and I told them that was exactly what we were going to do. I would sit with these two wonderful women as we bowed our heads together in prayer. My editor could wait.

> *The principle of family unity is dear to our family, and our values are clear.*

The principle of family unity is dear to our family, and our values are clear. It has been that way since long before I arrived on the scene. My grandfather on my mother's side of the family traveled to America to find good work and would return to Italy to share his earnings with his family. He, too, was a tailor.

Many of my relatives on my mom's side eventually came to America—and she was one of seven siblings. The rest of my father's family stayed in Italy. As I grew up on Long Island, I therefore had twenty-one first cousins nearby who were like brothers and sisters to me, though I was an only child. We lived within minutes of one another. Many hours away in Italy, across the waves, were my father's relatives, and we managed to visit with them every few years. They, too, became an important part of my life, and I spent lots of time with them.

I always felt, growing up, that I lived in a wealthy family, though we were far from rolling in money. All my needs were met. That was not what made us wealthy, though. We were dedicated to one another. We cared. From a young age, I observed that any one of us—my parents, my aunts and uncles, my cousins—would drop whatever he or she was doing on a moment's notice to be there for family. It was clearly demonstrated to me: that's what mattered most.

Today, in my immediate family, we have also strived to set the priorities that matter most. When Heather was running for school board, she chose to miss some campaign appearances on the last critical weekend so that she could attend my uncle's funeral. She ran the risk of losing the election so that she could pay her respects to my uncle and our cousins. Heather won anyway—and she also did the right thing. For her, the decision was easy: she honored our family. Both of us care deeply about our careers and our community outreach—and both of us know that we do it all for the sake of family.

We come now to the final section of this book, the "third cord" of family. This is where it all comes together. In the first section, we looked at personal development goals. In the second section, we talked about building a strong business. But what would be the point of any of that if your family fell apart? In fact, the point of everything that we have discussed thus far is to strengthen the very fibers of life so that your family bonds are as powerful as a triple-braided cord.

CHAPTER 7
RETIREMENT INCOME PLANNING

Retirement is like a long vacation in Vegas.
The goal is to enjoy these years to the fullest,
but not so fully that you run out of money.

—JONATHAN CLEMENTS

There it was, laid out in bold figures on the table in front of us. With my help, Jim and Donna were getting their first clear look at the full extent of their assets and income sources. Their business and investments had yielded them a net worth of over $50 million— and now, on the brink of retirement, they could see the possibilities. The couple lifted their eyes from the document, looked at me, and then at each other.

"Well," Donna told her husband, a sparkle in her eye, "I guess this means I really don't need you anymore!" Jim laughed. This was love. To say something like that, you must be either highly secure in your marriage or ready to bolt. There was something that this husband and wife clearly didn't need anymore, though. They did not need to keep accumulating. They had long since attained the financial independence to produce a substantial income for a lifetime without working another day if they chose not to do so. Jim and Donna needed each other. They just didn't need their business anymore.

It's a gratifying moment when I can lead a couple to that moment of clarity. I have found that many successful people have never paused long enough to get a good grasp of how much they own and the extent of their wealth and how it could be developed into a steady stream of reliable income. They feel surprised when they finally see those possibilities on paper.

This is your end game. As you get older, and you begin to anticipate retirement, it is high time that you know how much you have, where you are going with it, and how you will get there.

This is your end game. As you get older, and you begin to anticipate retirement, it is high time that you know how much you have, where you are going with it, and how you will get there. You launched a thriving enterprise, nurtured it for years, and now you have found a way to place it in worthy hands as you move on to other adventures.

Your dreams await. You have identified them, and you are ready to pursue them. How will you and your loved ones make the most of what you have amassed? How will your money translate into true family wealth? Life is about more than money, but money broadens horizons and expands prospects. You need a reliable income to see you through.

Income planning is an essential element of a comprehensive financial strategy. In previous chapters, we examined the importance of setting goals and objectives and of building wealth through the years. We looked at investment considerations while building a business and developing an exit strategy. In this chapter, we will examine more specifically what you should know as you go about turning the assets from your life's work into an income that will support your family's lifestyle and your pursuit of life's wonders still to come.

HOW MUCH WILL YOU NEED?

As you consider your family's ongoing income needs, be aware that retirees tend to spend more, not less, than they did during their working years. They have more time to travel. Frequently they want to do more and more things on behalf of their children and their grandchildren.

You may have heard that the typical spending in retirement is 80 percent of the previous level. That figure is often presented to prospective retirees as a guide to how much income they will need. What I have found, however, is that it is more like 110 to 120 percent. If you have been spending $150,000 a year, for example, you well might find yourself needing a net income of $180,000 in retirement.

Many people experience a spending surge in the early retirement years. They are rewarding themselves for all those decades of hard work. They are off to see the world or enjoy other experiences that they put off for so long. "We deserve this," they tell themselves, "and this is finally our time."

It's natural to want to spend a bit more in those years, and that is quite alright—so long as your resources are up to the task. We take a close look at whether your goals and your finances are a match. After several years, when all the trips are done and life resumes its regular course, the spending tends to taper off—although retirees tend to find plenty of things to do that money. Remember, once your working days are over, every day is like a weekend. Later in retirement, spending levels typically go up once again due to increased medical expenses.

Even people of significant wealth wonder how this major change of life will influence their family lifestyle. For most, this is a time when they become less willing to take on big risks. They adopt more of a protective stance with their wealth, although to be protective also means to guard against inflation. The retirement portfolio should attain at least enough growth to overcome that steady erosion, as well as the uncertainty of taxation.

The increased spending of those early years, as understandable as it might be, could pose a major problem if the retirement income is predicated on withdrawing money from an account that fluctuates with the financial markets. As you enter retirement, you may feel that you have plenty of assets to meet your family's needs. Unless you plan your withdrawals and spending carefully, however, that situation could change. You will do well to seek expert guidance to design an income plan for life.

SOURCES OF INCOME

You truly need to pay attention to the nature of your income sources. The money that you have set aside will be used for differing purposes, and therefore needs to be managed in different ways. A well-rounded income plan will include some money from guaranteed sources, such as Social Security benefits and annuities; sufficient liquid resources to cover emergencies and other needs and wants that might arise within a relatively short term; and some longer-term growth investments, as appropriate to the client's situation.

Within those parameters can be investments of many types. They might include IRA assets and non-IRA assets and real estate, for example. I must get to know the client and the family situation before I can make any recommendations. There is no income planning formula that covers everybody.

Much has been written about the amount that investors can withdraw annually from their account without running an undue risk of depleting it over time. Based on my experience, I put that figure at 3 percent for a typical client. That is the amount that is likely to work in any kind of market, including the downturn of 2008–2009.

Though that is the ideal, people often believe they can withdraw more, say 4 or 5.5 percent. Those withdrawals become particularly worrisome when they get much higher than that, to 6 or 8 or 10 percent, especially if a series of losing years comes early in retirement. Your portfolio may not be able to recover. That is the concept of sequence of returns.

Consider the math: If you have $1 million and take a 20 percent loss to $800,000, you might imagine that a 20 percent gain the next year would get you back to even. It would only get you back to $960,000—and that's presuming you made no withdrawals for income. If you took out 10 percent on top of the loss, that second year would only bring you up to $840,000.

You can see how your savings could dwindle during a few bad years up front. You would be far better off if you had a few good years to build up a cushion and the bad ones came later. You cannot count on that sequence, though, as you head into retirement. By keeping those withdrawal percentages down—perhaps by using funds that are not exposed to the market—you can significantly alleviate the risk.

The goal is to find the right balance of income and growth opportunity so that you can cover both your fixed and essential expenses and your discretionary or lifestyle ones. Which expenses fall into which category will differ from family to family. What you might consider optional, others will see as nonnegotiable. "How about wine?" more than one client has pointed out with a smile. "That's an essential expense, wouldn't you say?"

Individual investments have varying levels of three elements: preservation, liquidity, and growth. The investment mix determines how those qualities combine into a portfolio's ability to provide a reliable income. A well-crafted plan must provide a good balance of preservation, so that you have some income that is steady and more confidence that you will not run out of money; of liquidity, so that a portion of your money is reasonably accessible for emergencies and other uses; and of growth, so you can beat inflation and expand your portfolio to replenish your income needs and leave an appropriate inheritance.

In building your portfolio and income plan, you need to use the right investment product for the right purpose. Some investments are designed for growth, and others for stability, and each should be used as intended in a diversified mix. Where you are looking for more stability, for example, a risky stock is not your best choice. Where you are looking for significant growth that will outpace inflation, a CD or bank account is not going to deliver to your expectations. And you should not lock up money to which you may soon need easy access into illiquid investments such as your IRA or real estate.

Diversification to reduce risk is a key element of modern portfolio theory, which holds that for a given level of risk, you can design a portfolio to increase the possible return. Failure to diversify can lead to dire financial consequences, as many investors learned during the Great Recession. To prevent so many retirees from being forced to sell at a loss in 2009, Congress voted to let them skip their required IRA distributions that year. The economic slump was particularly hard on investors who had failed to diversify.

TAKING IT STEP BY STEP

As you and your advisor design an income plan for a secure retirement, you will begin by taking a snapshot of your current financial picture. That is the first step. You need to see clearly where you stand today. What is your condition "as is"? You should know just how much you have in the way of assets, and how that compares to the amount you owe in debt.

The next step is to get a good grasp on your fixed and variable expenses so that you can size up your goals. When you know how you are spending your money and understand how much is for essential needs and how much is for optional wants, you will see more clearly whether your goals are realistic and attainable. How much are you spending on each? Is that level of spending compromising your objectives? At this point, you are looking beyond the "as is" to get a view of the "should be."

Once you know your destination and feel confident that you have enough fuel to get there, the next step is to work out your roadmap. You need to develop a plan and know how you will execute on it. It is time to identify all the challenges that you are likely to face along the way. And as you get started, ask yourself these questions: What will this mean to you once you accomplish it? Personally, how much importance do you attach to achieving your overall financial goals? Do you feel gratified to be doing what is right on behalf of your family? This is a matter of motivation. You will succeed if you are convinced that these steps are essential to your pursuit of happiness.

YOUR MONEY BUCKETS

When my clients and I get to the point of executing on a plan, I sometimes will explain the importance of asset allocation by asking them to imagine that they are putting their money into several pools, or buckets. They will be investing the money in each of those buckets differently than they do in the others.

What to put in each bucket and how best to manage it will vary depending on the client's needs and aspirations, but generally these will be separate buckets for immediate or emergency needs, for short-term spending and living expenses, and for longer-term purposes.

The first bucket is to ensure that you have a proper cash reserve of liquid assets for use in emergencies or to take advantage of opportunities. It should be big enough to cover between three months and a year's worth of expenses.

The second bucket should contain money that you are unlikely to need for three to seven years. Those should be fixed income investments of a relatively short term. You could draw from that bucket during times when the equity market environment is troubled.

Other money would be put into the third, longer-term buckets. Invested in the market for growth, these are assets that you likely would not use for many years. When necessary, this money also can replenish your shorter-term spending buckets.

In general, the bucket system works like this: The sooner you will need the money, the less you should subject it to risk. If you need it right away, or might need it right away, it should be in a low-risk, accessible account. If you do not anticipate needing it for a few years, you can invest it at moderate risk. If you won't need the money for quite some time, if ever, you can take on even more risk. That is because your longer-term account will have time to recover if the market sinks—that is, if you are not hitting it when it is down by using it for your living expenses.

The bucket system of retirement income planning greatly reduces the sequence of return risk that can present such a danger when bad years come early in retirement. You will be able to weather a bear market because you will not be deriving your immediate income from money invested in equities. Because you have already accounted for your income needs, you will not have to dip into the money you set aside for growth. You can leave it alone as it recovers to grow anew. Remember: diversified investors did not lose a cent in the crashes of 1929, 1987, or 2008, or any other downturn, so long as they did not sell, because losses are only realized once the investments are sold. By structuring your income long before such a storm, you will be positioning yourself, and your family, for success.

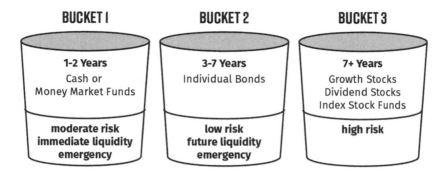

WHAT YOU NEED TO KNOW

→ Despite the common perception, retirees tend to spend more, not less, than they did during their working years.

→ The money that you have set aside will be used for differing purposes, and therefore needs to be managed in different ways.

→ The first step in income planning is to know your current financial picture. The second step is to know your fixed and variable expenses to determine if your goals are realistic. The third step is to work out a roadmap to reach your goals.

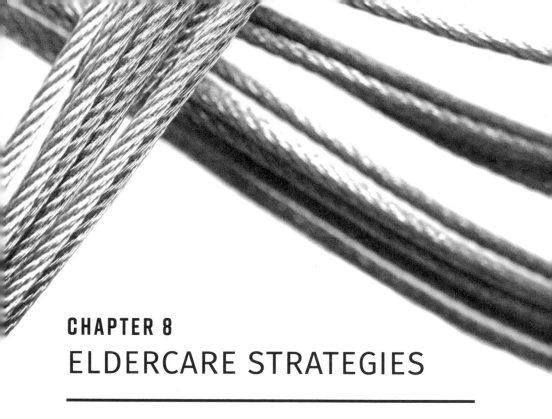

CHAPTER 8
ELDERCARE STRATEGIES

*America's healthcare system is neither
healthy, caring, nor a system.*

—WALTER CRONKITE

In the 1995 movie *Above Suspicion*, Christopher Reeve portrayed a paraplegic police officer. To play the role more authentically, the actor visited a rehabilitation center before and during the filming. He wanted to understand what paraplegics must endure. A few months after he finished the film, an equestrian accident left him paralyzed from the neck down. He required constant care for nine years, until his death in 2004.

Every time he left that rehab center as he was preparing for his movie, Reeve told Oprah Winfrey a few years after the accident, "I would think, *Thank God that's not me.*" He regretted that he had felt so smug, so complacent. "We're all one great big family," he said, "and any one of us can get hurt at any moment"—even when you are young, and even if you are like Superman.

Nonetheless, many people do not anticipate the risk of needing extended care. "These are things that happen to other people," they often think—but, as Reeve put it, "anything can happen to anybody." And though the need can arise suddenly, from an accident or medical crisis, more commonly people require an increasing level of assistance as they get older.

Eldercare is certain to become an increasing need in our society. How real is this risk? The National Association of Insurance Commissioners (NAIC) recently projected that more than a third of U.S. residents who reach age sixty-five will need to enter an extended care facility at some point. The average stay is a year. Twice as many, about 70 percent, are expected to need long-term care assistance in some form, the NAIC projects.[14]

---

14 "National Association of Insurance Commissioners, *A Shopper's Guide to Long-Term Care Insurance*," National Association of Insurance Commissioners, 2013, http://www.naic.org/documents/prod_serv_consumer_ltc_lp.pdf.

Our nation is aging, and within forty years we will have eighteen million people age eighty-five and older, nearly triple today's number, according to the Census Bureau.[15] The increasing need for long-term care—and the financial risk that it entails—is undeniable. You run the risk that years of costly care could devastate your family financially. In one way or another, you should arrange to protect yourself and your loved ones from that threat.

I had a client who made his living in the insurance industry but kept telling me that he did not need long-term care insurance, though I repeatedly encouraged him to get it. If he changed his mind, he told me, he could readily acquire it. He never did. He entered a nursing home, and the expense depleted most of the retirement assets that he and his wife had set aside. Much of their savings was in an IRA account, and so for every $14,000 a month that the facility charged, they had to withdraw $19,000 to cover the taxes as well. His wife was in a tough financial situation when he died. According to AARP, in 2020 on Long Island, nursing home costs on an annual basis could reach $190,000 per year.[16]

15   Jennifer M. Ortman, Victoria A. Velkoff, and Howard Hogan, "*An Aging Nation: The Older Population in the United States, Current Population Reports,*" U.S. Census Bureau, 2014, https://www.census.gov/prod/2014pubs/p25-1140.pdf.

16   Ellen Stark, "Five Things You Should Know about Long-Term Care Insurance," AARP Bulletin, March 2018, https://www.aarp.org/caregiving/financial-legal/info-2018/long-term-care-insurance-fd.html.

IT'S TIME TO TALK ABOUT IT

The need for long-term care is not something that is likely to come up casually in a family conversation, even between spouses. It's human nature: We do not want to imagine ourselves in such a condition. We would like to be vigorous, astute, and self-reliant to the end. Those who have experienced a loved one's physical or mental decline are more likely to understand why they should acquire financial protection against the cost of care. Sometimes, dying takes years.

Meanwhile, life savings can evaporate. It does not need to be that way. The infirmities of aging are, to some extent, inevitable, and therefore a comprehensive financial plan should anticipate this cost of care. No matter how hard, it's time to talk about it.

Sometimes, husbands and wives will presume that if one of them is in need, the other will be the caregiver. Or they may suppose that their grown children will be able to fill that role. In another day and age, that was common. When my great grand-mother in Italy was no longer able to care for herself, she came to America, where my mother and my two aunts took turns looking after her. She lived at each home for a few years at a time until she died at age ninety-four.

My mom and aunts, though, did not have careers outside the house. For many families today, that kind of home care is increasingly impractical. Often the children are busy pursuing their own business and family obligations. Though they are loving and loyal to mom and dad, the logistics are daunting. And in this age of medical complexity, caregiving requires more than dedication and physical and emotional stamina. In many cases, it calls for clinical skills that most people lack.

The default plan for countless families is that they somehow will deal with this need if it should arise, but otherwise they do nothing. Some affluent families do have the capacity to pay out-of-pocket. Essentially, they self-insure. They have the means to set aside sufficient assets that they earmark for long-term care if that need should arise for one or both spouses. If you are in that league, be aware that this expense could amount to hundreds of thousands of dollars.

Most families instead will need to insure against the long-term care risk.

THE GOVERNMENT AS CARETAKER

Rather than protect against the need for long-term care, a common but questionable approach is to try to let the government be the caretaker. Some look to the Medicare and Medicaid programs to pay for their needs so that they can protect their life savings. It does not work that way. Medicare is designed to cover only the bare minimum of such expenses for a brief period. Medicaid is a program for those in need. It helps you only if you establish that you have low or no income.

Medicare will pay for only a hundred days of rehab care if you are transferred to an approved facility from a hospital. After that, the care is considered to be long term, and you are expected to pay the tab. If you have the resources, you will need to spend most of that money first for your care before becoming eligible for the state-based Medicaid system. You can keep a few things, depending on the regulations of your state. You probably will be able to keep your house, car, personal belongings, and a minimal amount of other assets. Family income will be strictly limited. Your required withdrawals from a retirement plan could make you ineligible.

Some people make themselves eligible for Medicaid by transferring assets to family members or into a trust. That way, they technically have little in the way of their own resources and can qualify for the welfare assistance. If that is the way you want to go, you will need to start the planning at least five years in advance. That is how far back the government will be examining your assets to see what you transferred. It's called the "look-back" period. If the government discovers that you took assets out of your name during that time, it will assume you were trying to qualify for Medicaid. You will not get coverage until you contribute that amount toward your care.

Be aware, though, that when you submit to the government's caretaking, you could be placed in a state facility far from your loved ones, depending on where a room is available. A state program may not provide you with the quality of care that you would desire. Medicaid facilities and services may fall far short of expectations. Sometimes the children who received assets under a Medicaid strategy will transfer that money back out of the trust in order to pay for something better for mom or dad.

INSURANCE SOLUTIONS

Even those who have the resources to potentially self-insure should consider the power of insurance to leverage their dollars. That insurance could come in the form of a traditional long-term care policy, or as a rider for long-term care on a life insurance policy or annuity.

Some people are reluctant to get insurance because they do not want to pay those premiums for a service that they may never need. They are concerned that the money spent on those premiums will be wasted—but how is that different than paying for auto or homeowners insurance? They are not exactly eager to pay for car repairs or a new roof after a storm, either, but they don't consider those premiums wasted when such troubles come. What they are buying with insurance is protection against the possibility of a burdensome expense.

Traditional long-term care insurance can help greatly with the expenses, although you should shop carefully for the right provider and the right policy. In recent years, some policyholders have been shocked to see their premiums increasing by a third, or even two-thirds, as the insurance companies get a grip on the real risks involved. They miscalculated earlier policies, and now some retirees find themselves unable to afford the new rates. Some paid their premiums faithfully for years and then had to drop their coverage just as they were getting closer to potentially needing the services. They may have been under the illusion that their premiums were guaranteed not to rise, but that was not the case.

When it works well, though, traditional long-term care insurance provides a terrific benefit, and facilities could give preference for admission to those who have it. Families may wish to gauge how much insurance they need based on the typical length of stay in a nursing home, which usually does not exceed two or three years—though it might only be a few months, or it could last several years. Because they cannot know for certain, many families play the odds. They structure a plan to cover care either at home or in a facility, with a benefit sufficient to pay for perhaps three years of the typical cost in their region.

An alternative strategy is to acquire a life insurance policy or annuity with provisions that provide long-term care benefits. Some life insurance policies offer an early distribution of the death benefit if it is needed for long-term care. If you never need it, the benefit instead goes to your heirs. Some annuities also include long-term care provisions. For example, if you meet the criteria for care, the annuity could double your monthly cash payments.

Some families prefer those types of insurance products because they get a level of protection but still see their money working for them. They feel reassured that they or their loved ones will at least get something back from those premiums. The amount of coverage may fall short of their financial needs if they need nursing home care, but it will certainly be a help.

Many families take a combination approach. They may decide to self-insure up to a certain level, while also acquiring some form of insurance to cover the remaining amount that they most likely will face. If they anticipate a cost of $400 a day, they may decide to pay $200 out of pocket and purchase insurance to cover the rest. Or a couple may wish to set aside a piece of real estate that they could liquidate in the event that one or both of them needed care. By doing so, they can feel reassured that they have acted responsibly and accounted for that contingency. However, they may also recognize that long-term care insurance not only protects themselves but also may relieve some stress and responsibility for their heirs.

In other words, by leveraging dollars through insurance, you could leave more for your loved ones. In some families, the children pay for the policy on their parents out of a sense of gratitude for what they will inherit and out of a desire to see mom and dad get the best. The family members talk it through, identify the ultimate goal, and take the steps together to make it happen.

WHAT YOU NEED TO KNOW

→ Years of expensive care can be financially devastating, costing hundreds of thousands of dollars. You should arrange to protect yourself and your loved ones from that threat.

→ In this age of medical complexity, caregiving probably is not a job for your spouse or children. It requires more than dedication and stamina. In many cases, it calls for clinical skills that most people lack.

→ Even if you are wealthy enough to pay out-of-pocket, you should consider the power of insurance to leverage your dollars. That insurance could come in the form of a traditional long-term care policy, or as a rider for long-term care on a life insurance policy or annuity.

CHAPTER 9
ESTATE AND LEGACY PLANNING

*Planning is bringing the future into the present
so that you can do something about it now.*

—ALAN LAKEIN

Fresh out of college, Tony got a great position at a Fortune 500 company and married his sweetheart, Carla. Soon after starting his new job, he filled out all the requisite paperwork for his pension plan, listing Carla as his beneficiary. Within a year, their relationship soured and they soon divorced. They had no children and made what seemed like a clean break. Carla moved to Montana, and Tony never saw her again.

Tony thrived at that company and married one of his college friends, Elizabeth. They raised three children together, and their marriage was ideal. As the family grew, Tony visited a lawyer and drafted a will and a trust. He wanted everything to go smoothly in case something were to happen to him. Over the years, the retirement account grew.

Thirty years later, Tony died of a heart attack while shoveling snow. After the funeral, Elizabeth arranged to roll over the pension account to her name with their children to be the beneficiaries. "Yes, here it is," the account custodian said, peering at the old paperwork to find the beneficiary designation. "But he left it to someone named Carla."

Carla was alive and well, and the account custodian was legally obligated to contact her about the situation. Elizabeth imagined that perhaps Carla would say something like "Oh, that's okay, this is just a misunderstanding. Tony obviously meant all that money for you. After all, we were married only a year or so." That wasn't exactly her attitude, though. Instead, she claimed all the inheritance. "If he had intended to change this, he would have done so at some point over these three decades," Carla said. "He clearly wanted me to have the money."

Generally, neither a will nor a trust will supersede a beneficiary form, whether it's for a retirement plan or insurance policy or annuity or another financial instrument. Nor can those legal documents overturn the titled ownership of property, such as the deed to a house. Once you have passed away, the courts have no choice but to enforce the documentation on record. Sometimes, young people starting a job list their parents as beneficiaries. Then they marry and neglect to change the beneficiary to the spouse. It's a setup for a surprise someday—either a pleasant or unpleasant one, depending on one's perspective.

It costs nothing to update your beneficiaries, but it could cost you a fortune if you fail to do it. That is why a beneficiary review is an essential and regular part of the services that I provide for my clients as we monitor their comprehensive financial plans. We conduct a full examination annually. I need to know whether anything has changed in your life or your family that would influence how you would wish to transfer assets in all your financial instruments, including your trust and other estate planning documents.

AN ORDERLY ESTATE AND LEGACY PLAN

Elizabeth's nightmare scenario underscores the importance of thorough planning and continued vigilance when managing your family estate plan. One day you will be gone, and your loved ones will need your affairs to be in order.

Even if you never give a thought to creating an estate plan, you can be sure that you have one by default. The government will create one for you. If you have taken no action to decide what will become of your life's work, the state will do that for you. The judge and lawyers will figure it out through the probate process—but what they decide will probably not be what you would have preferred. Probate gets expensive and time consuming.

Most people want better. They want more control over the transfer of their estate. They want to decide just who will get the assets, whether family or charity, and how and when it will happen.

The better and more efficient way is a carefully designed estate plan that is tax efficient and may keep private family affairs away from public scrutiny.

Take the case of the recording artist Prince as an example of how not to do your estate planning. Prince, who died of an accidental overdose of an opioid painkiller, was known to be a very private man, concerned about controlling his image and publicity. However, the singer never drafted a will, or a trust, or any documents for wealth transfer. His estate therefore was destined to go through probate court. No privacy there. All the details got plenty of publicity, and the government assumed the control, ready to reap millions in taxes.

As is the case with long-term care planning, estate planning can be a difficult topic to contemplate. Again, we are talking about the end of a life. Few people are eager to dive into such a conversation, and it is tempting to procrastinate. But we are also talking about beginnings. We are talking about what will work best for the next generation. You have spent decades building your business interests and acquiring assets. You did it for your family—and now you will want to follow through so that everything falls into place.

The technicalities of estate planning, however, are just part of what you should be addressing as you consider what you will leave behind. You are bequeathing to your family much more than the money and the property. Your values and your principles will be part of their inheritance, as well. As you write your final chapter, you will want to ensure that your

> *You are bequeathing to your family much more than the money and the property. Your values and your principles will be part of their inheritance, as well.*

life story continues into an epilogue for the generations to come. Estate planning therefore should be a companion to charitable and legacy planning.

These are the central questions of estate and legacy planning: Do you wish to make the most of your money while you are alive, so that you can enhance your lifestyle, or do you want to leave as much as you can to your children and other heirs, or to charity? If you want to leave a sizable sum, then how much will go to family and how much to the causes and institutions that are important to you? What are the tax implications of your decisions? Does anyone in your family have a special need that you wish to support?

These are the central questions of estate and legacy planning: Do you wish to make the most of your money while you are alive, so that you can enhance your lifestyle, or do you want to leave as much as you can to your children and other heirs, or to charity?

As I get to know my clients, we discuss such matters. I first need to know their legacy aspirations so that we can calculate how much money will be available for their use while they are alive and the best way to produce a lifelong income. Often, some form of insurance will play into the equation. Many families, for example, find that it makes more sense to pay premiums on a life insurance policy than to try to grow the portfolio by an amount equivalent to the death benefit. In effect, and subject to a few exceptions, the death benefit is a tax-free payout to your beneficiaries in an amount that you designate, with the remainder of your assets available for your use during retirement. In addition, if you are leaving your business to one of your children, the insurance payout can equalize your estate for your other children.

Generally, it is a good idea to speak openly with your grown children about such matters, to the extent that you feel is appropriate. If you want the kids to know your intentions, you should include them in meetings to review the situation, and they can be present for discussions with the estate planning attorney to make sure everyone is on board with the decisions. That way, nothing will be coming as a surprise. Some people by nature are more private about

A well-designed estate plan will give you and your family a sense of confidence in the future. Knowing how much you have set aside for which purposes, you will not need to worry about whether you are overspending or underspending. Your legacy goals are much like your life achievement goals: only when you have clearly identified them will you know how to design a plan to meet them.

their money and their assets, and you don't have to tell your family everything—but it's good for them to know that you do have a plan and whom you are working with. That helps greatly with the continuity when it comes time to transition the assets.

A well-designed estate plan will give you and your family a sense of confidence in the future. Knowing how much you have set aside for which purposes, you will not need to worry about whether you are overspending or underspending. Your legacy goals are much like your life achievement goals: only when you have clearly identified them will you know how to design a plan to meet them.

THE ESTATE PLANNING BASICS

You will have no trouble finding detailed information from many sources on the various common documents of estate planning, but let's look at several of the primary ones that you will want to consider. These are documents that you should prepare with the help of an attorney who specializes in them. The legal language needs to be specific and tailored precisely to your family situation. I can help to coordinate your planning and communicate your unique needs to the right professional.

Will

Your last will and testament is the most basic vehicle for passing assets to your children, other heirs, or charities. If you have young children, this document should also name a guardian. In your will, you name an executor who will file the document in probate court when you die, and who will then work with the court to distribute your assets as you have specified. You should choose that person with care; you need someone with the knowledge and stamina to complete what can be a detailed and arduous task. Your executor will be responsible for ensuring the payment of all taxes, debts, and expenses. These distributions will be a matter of public record in probate court.

Revocable living trust

If you want to manage your estate planning while you are alive, you will need more than a will. With a revocable living trust, you can set up provisions to manage your affairs if you become incapable of doing so. You can change those provisions at any time, and if you act as your own trustee you will be able to continue managing your investments and financial affairs. The terms of the trust remain in force after your death. You can stipulate, for example, exactly how you wish your assets to be distributed, and a well-designed trust can protect against claims by creditors and litigators. The provisions and stipulations of your trust can extend your influence for generations.

Durable power of attorney

You should designate someone who has the power to act on your behalf if you cannot. That is the purpose of a durable power of attorney. You will be giving someone whom you trust the authority and discretion to manage and invest your assets to the extent that you decide is appropriate. It is called a durable power because it endures throughout the time that you are incapacitated. It does not extend beyond your death, however.

Health care power of attorney

You should grant another power of attorney, as well: someone should have the specific authority to make medical decisions on your behalf if you are unable. Families often feel divided over what should be the best course of medical care. Sometimes they go to court over such matters. You can shortstop such dissension by legally designating who will decide.

Advance medical directive

Some people are appalled at the thought that they might linger for weeks, or years, hooked up to life support and unable to communicate. They want to be certain that the doctors understand their desires for end-of-life care. To avoid the possibility that you will be kept alive against your wishes, you can file what is often called a "living will" with your health care providers. This is an advance medical directive that states your desires. The doctors will be able to abide by your wishes with less concern that they will be held liable. The living will differs from a health care power of attorney in that it does not give anyone else the right to make decisions on your behalf.

ADVANTAGES OF A TRUST

Affluent families will want to pay particularly close attention to the importance of the trust because of its usefulness in managing estate taxes, but by no means is that the only reason to consider establishing and funding one.

The 2018 exemption for federal estate taxes is $11.2 million per person, or up to nearly $22.4 million for a couple. In other words, they can leave that much to their heirs without paying any federal estate or gift tax. Only the value of their estate above that amount would be subject to tax at the federal level. The exemption is the same in many states, although in some it is not nearly as much of a break. Nonetheless, family estates can easily exceed those thresholds. Half of any amount above the exemption could go to the government instead of to the heirs. To avoid that, many families of means will utilize a trust to keep a portion of their holdings out of the estate.

Trusts are useful for controlling much more than taxes, however. You can include stipulations on who will get which assets, and you can specify how they will be allowed to spend it. An attorney can even help you carefully set up a trust to become the designated beneficiary for your retirement plan or insurance benefit. That will keep those payouts from passing directly to your children or other heirs so that you can place limitations and restrictions on how they handle it.

For example, you may want the recipients to receive only a small percentage of the account every year, or to get only the interest earned but none of the principal. You may wish to earmark the money for use only to establish a business, or to buy a first house, or to pay for educational costs. Perhaps you have a spendthrift in your family to whom you still wish to offer support—but only when he or she gets the nod of a trusted person of your choosing.

Perhaps you have a special needs child and want to arrange for lifelong care, establishing precisely how that money can be spent through the years.

Only a trust can give you that level of control. You cannot do it with a will. You cannot add some sort of notation to a beneficiary designation. If you wish to maintain control of your family assets long after your passing, you can do so only with the provisions of a trust. It is your way to make sure that your life's work is put to good use. You will be doing right by your family.

CHARITABLE INTENTIONS

Those who wish to leave a legacy often want to help charities as well as their children. They may believe that they can do one or the other but not both, but that is certainly not so. You can set up a charitable giving plan that gives generously to both. Only the tax collector loses out.

Various trusts are specifically designed for charitable giving. For example, many families and business owners with large estates set up charitable remainder trusts and charitable lead trusts. With the charitable remainder trust, you continue to get the interest income from the value of your contribution during your lifetime, and after you die your chosen charity gets the remainder. With a charitable lead trust, the charity gets the interest income from the value of your contribution during your lifetime or for a set number of years, but your family or other heirs will still inherit the asset. Even if you are not inclined to give to charity, those trusts are worthwhile for their tax benefits. Otherwise, the government will claim a greater share and distribute it for whatever purposes it deems best. This way, you make that decision.

Once you have made the decision to give to charity, you and your advisor should identify which of your assets are fully taxable. That's what you should donate to charities, which are exempt from taxation. For example, if you leave money from your IRA or 401(k) to your children, they must pay all the deferred tax. If you donate it, the charity receives it tax-free, and that amount will not become taxable to your estate. What you instead could leave to your children are nontaxable assets such as proceeds from a life insurance policy. You can also leave them assets for which they get a step-up in basis. In other words, they inherit those assets based on what they are worth at the time of your death, not what they were worth when you acquired them, and therefore they will not be taxed on the capital gains during those years. The step-up in basis would be pointless for a charity since it faces no tax anyway.

A donor-advised fund is a convenient tool that many families use for charitable giving. You get an immediate tax deduction for whatever you put into the fund each year. The money then stays in the account and you can continue to invest and have it managed until you later decide how you will distribute it to charity. You do not donate. You request a grant to an organization. You can only advise where the money should go. The sponsoring organization has control over the assets once contributed, so it is possible that they could ignore the contributor's request. A donor advised fund simplifies tax preparation because you do not have to file separate forms for each charity. You file just one form for the fund, and you have a convenient record of your donations through the years.

RICHES BEYOND MONEY

When people say that they have led a rich life, they generally do not mean that they are romping through their days extravagantly with money to burn. They are saying that they appreciate that they have been blessed with another kind of wealth—a life rich in relationships, and values, and family bonds. These are the riches beyond money that many people are eager to leave to the next generations. Yes, they want to efficiently pass on their money, but they want to pass on something less tangible, too, and that is the story of their life and what they have found meaningful.

Estate planning entails a variety of practical and tax considerations, but much of it rests on a foundation of building a legacy. Many people, as they get older, begin to think deeply about the causes they cherish and the institutions they admire. They often increasingly engage in volunteer work, demonstrating what matters most to them. They know that their legacy will be measured in more than financial terms. They want to be remembered as more than a shrewd investor who knew how to handle a dollar. They want to be remembered by matters of the heart.

While I don't always keep up with it every day, I have long kept a journal of life experiences and write an annual essay of observations and aspirations. Some people make audio or video recordings. These can be precious gifts to those you leave behind. In doing so, you will be sharing your sentiments with descendants yet to be born. You will become more than just a name that they might have heard. They will know your story. You will be creating a family history that can include a chronology of events, an appreciation of those you love, and a clear communication of your values and your dreams. If you have built a business, you can explain why you did it. What did it mean to you? What did you wish to accomplish for your family?

Much of your legacy will be in the memories you create along the way. Your family traditions will outlive you. They are what your grandchildren will be sharing one day with their own grandchildren. In recent years, I have scheduled special dad-and-daughter weekends with Ella, and now that Luca is old enough, I am doing weekends with him, too. When Ella was turning ten, we visited the city and went on a helicopter ride around Manhattan. We dined at the Sugar Factory and went to a Broadway show and to the Central Park Zoo. For Luca, we went to a Mets game, the Lego store, and had dinner at Ninja Cafe. Our family looks forward to a movie night on Fridays, and going to Nonna's house for Sunday pasta dinner, and spending Christmas Eve with the whole family. Those are the occasions, and the moments—some special, some routine—that shape the heart.

It all comes back to family. I spend a lot of time working with people on how to manage their financial resources, but if making money is their only objective, I fear that they will die sad someday. We do what we do for the sake of those we love. That's why we build our businesses, that's why we set goals and plan for a better future, and that's why we take good care of ourselves. In the end, what will be important is whether we truly invested in what matters.

WHAT YOU NEED TO KNOW

→ If you never develop an estate plan, you will have one by default. The judge and lawyers will figure it out in probate court, which gets time consuming and expensive.

→ The basic documents of an estate plan include a will, a revocable living trust, a durable power of attorney, a health care power of attorney, and an advance medical directive.

→ This is your legacy. You are bequeathing to your family much more than the money and the property. Your values and your principles will be part of their inheritance, as well.

CONCLUSION
TYING THE CORDS TOGETHER

It is easy to sit up and take notice. What is difficult is getting up and taking action.

—HONORÉ DE BALZAC

Real estate developer Ken Behring, author of *Road to Purpose*, says he spent years trying to find happiness by acquiring "stuff"— houses, cars, boats, airplanes, even an NFL football team. None of it worked. Then a friend invited him on a flight to Europe to give away wheelchairs to children in need. He was so touched by their appreciation that he founded the Wheelchair Foundation, which has since given away hundreds of thousands of wheelchairs to children and adults worldwide. During a trip to Mexico, after Behring lifted a boy into his new chair, the child told him he wanted to memorize his face so that he could thank him again when they met in heaven. It was a moment, Behring says, of sheer joy. He had never felt so wealthy.

I am a financial advisor. I help people manage and grow their money, but I also help them recognize ways to fit it into their lives so that they can fulfill dreams. You will hear many perspectives on the meaning of true wealth. Some would say that you are wealthy when you have good health, particularly if they have lost it. Some would say that you are wealthy if you have a great family life, particularly if theirs is lacking. You can be rich even if you have relatively little money—and you can have multimillions but not be rich.

> *We need to set worthy goals and pursue objectives instead of just ambling along in the moment.*

Yes, it's good to grow your fortune, because money opens a world of possibilities. It lets you do more, and reach out more to others. I think of money as a great emphasizer. If you are a caring, generous person, money serves to emphasize those qualities in you. If you are mean and selfish, however, money will emphasize those traits, too.

We must be careful, therefore, about how we channel that power. We need to set worthy goals and pursue objectives instead of just ambling along in the moment. How will you conduct your business in this world? Is your intent to just make more and more money, or is your goal to serve others? And if you are selling a business, what next? Have you defined your purpose for the years to come? Do you have a vision for how you can put those dollars to work? To whom much has been given, much is expected. When we give back, we are repaid in dividends of happiness.

One of my clients, a wealthy businessman, told me after he sold his company that he intended to forgive the various private loans he had given to members of his family, and his thoughts have turned to what he might do in the community to help others. He has decided to do as much good as he can with his money— because, after all, you can't take it with you. His attitude reminds me of Andrew Carnegie, who became fabulously wealthy in the steel industry and spent his later years giving much of it to philanthropic causes centered on education and world peace.

Managing your money well, so that it can do the most good for your family and for the community, is a huge responsibility.

You want to do this right. This is not something to approach casually. You should be working with a professional with whom you can develop a rapport and who will be at your side for years to come. Most successful businesspeople understand the need to delegate to trusted colleagues with specialized skills. Money management is a specialized skill, and you should consult regularly with someone who has your back. In my relationships with my clients, I often feel as if I am an extension of their families.

> *Managing your money well, so that it can do the most good for your family and for the community, is a huge responsibility. You want to do this right.*

My hope, as you put down this book, is that you will always keep in mind the power of the three cords. Your personal interests, your business interests, and your family interests are all part of the fabric of your life. You must not separate them. You need to take care of yourself so that you can take care of your business so that you can take care of your family. Those three cords, braided together, will give you a rope that you can climb, or pull, or throw out to others as a lifeline. By attending to them all, you will gain the strength for success.